Manipulation and Dark Psychology

(2 Book Box Set)

R.J. Anderson

Table of Contents

Book #1 – Dark Psychology

Book #2 - Manipulation

Dark Psychology

Master the Advanced Secrets of Psychological Warfare,
Covert Persuasion, Dark NLP, Stealth Mind Control,
Dark Cognitive Behavioral Therapy, Maximum
Manipulation, and Human Psychology

Introduction

This book is slightly evil and semi-sociopathic. The techniques are evil and can be used to gain advantages over others. I am revealing all the secrets I've used or learned over my lifetime.

There is nothing inherently evil about knowledge. You can use this knowledge to defend yourself from others and also easily use it for personal gain. You can use this info to persuade and influence people for both benign and nefarious purposes.

It's no secret that our world is screwed up. The rules are designed to keep you down and in check, but I can show you how to get around those rules and see the rat race for what it is: a carefully designed and maintained empire of control.

These techniques are simply tools—tools that allow you to control people, often without their knowledge. Others know of these techniques and use them against people at great personal risk. Use this information cautiously or you may suffer the consequences.

But just because I'm showing you how to be evil doesn't mean we can't keep things professional. Evil is surprisingly professional and clear about its intentions. I go straight to the point with actionable tips and make it easy to follow.

Each chapter dives deep into one topic. No BS fillers! I get straight to the point with examples and practical tips about how these techniques are used.

Chapter 1: Persuasion

Persuasion is the process by which a person's attitudes or behavior are, without duress, influenced by communication from other people. One's attitude and behavior are also affected by other factors (e.g. verbal threats, physical coercion, or one's physiological states).

I've spent decades learning how human nature works. The way our mind processes arguments and stores facts is fascinating. In that time, I've come to some conclusions about what is and isn't persuasive.

It doesn't really matter what the content of your message is. The goal of any interaction isn't to be right, or to even prove the other person wrong. The real goal is to convince the other person that your interpretation of the facts is the right one.

Getting people to serve your dark will is a lot easier than it seems. You just have to know how to present their options in a way that makes your plan the best possible solution to whatever crisis your victims find themselves in.

Remember that there is a difference between persuasion and manipulation. It may seem small but it makes a world of difference when people find out. There are three main areas where persuasion moves into manipulation.

How to tell if you are manipulative or persuasive:

Intent: If your intention is to fool your victim, it's manipulation. People normally react poorly when they find out they are being manipulated. So when you try to convince someone of something, make a big deal about how your intention is to help them.

> **Example:** "I'm only saying this now to save you the pain of finding out later."

Truthfulness: If you lie, it's manipulation. People hate getting lied to. So whenever you are trying to be persuasive, make sure to include enough truth to have plausible deniability.

> **Example:** "Why would I do something like that? You know I hate the cold. But Dave always talks about how he never needs a coat."

Impact: If there is no true benefit for the person, it is manipulation. When you influence people, they will want to blame you if it doesn't work out in their interest. Make sure to play up the impact of others to distance yourself from responsibility for the negative consequences of following your advice.

> **Example:** "Your wife never gives you any room, Dan. You know, Greg's wife is the same way but he really showed her who's boss when he came home with a convertible instead of a mini-van. I bet he would tell you to go for the convertible if he were here right now."

9

It's important to keep the big picture in mind. But highly persuasive people also employ specific techniques to improve their ability to influence others. By improving each of these areas, you increase the chance that your attempts to persuade will work.

Take Bold Stands: Research shows that people prefer cockiness to expertise.

The brain is designed to equate confidence with skill. Even in the face of overwhelming evidence, the right amount of confidence will make people forgive or explain away previous failures.

People prefer confidence so much that I can override almost any expert opinion with little to no personal experience. Add some enthusiasm and an unwavering belief that my position is the best position, and it really turns up the pressure.

I avoid statements like "I believe" and "I think." Instead, I use statements like "The reality is" and "I know." Whatever happens, standing behind my opinions makes others question themselves first.

Adjust Speech Rates: Salesmen talk faster than preachers for a reason.

In situations where your audience/victim is likely to disagree, speaking faster can improve your persuasiveness. It makes sure they don't have time to weigh and react to everything you say.

This makes them more likely to go with their "gut feeling" and let themselves be convinced.

But fast talking doesn't work as well if the subjects are likely to agree with me. Speaking slower lets my words sink in and reaffirm their mental bias, but I also make sure to talk fast enough to keep their attention.

Start with Small Wins: Agreement is cumulative.

Repeatedly thinking the same thing strengthens the neural pathways used for that thought and actively trims the others. This makes thought patterns like ruts in the road—the more traveled they are, the easier it is to follow them.

This technique reaches peak effectiveness after three or more similar responses. Agreements are more commonly used, but people are just as susceptible to negative wins as well. So effective persuaders wait to reveal their main point until they get three or more responses in a row that align with their intentions.

> **Example:** "You love your wife, right? She deserves the best, right? You would do anything to make her happy, right? Well joining the Legion as a superhero training dummy comes with insurance that covers radiation therapy for her rare medical condition."

Swear Occasionally: Swearing shows passion.

This doesn't mean I swear at every opportunity. That just makes me look vulgar and weak. But a properly timed and heart-fucking-felt swear will show everybody I feel strongly about the topic.

It additionally gives the air of authenticity to whatever I am swearing about. This can be enough to dissuade dissent among peers and subordinates. This only increases buy-in slightly so I don't rely on it as the only way to get out of trouble.

> **Example:** "James, I understand that this is a hot topic for you, but sit the fuck down and listen to what we have to say."

Know How People Process Info: Pastors and scientists see the world differently.

Trying to convince a scientist that the world was created by God can be tough. The opposite is true as well because of how each person views the world and interprets information. I tailor my words and approach to the person I am trying to persuade to get the maximum impact.

When influencing someone religious, I use words like "faith" and "plan". When I need a scientist to agree, I use words like "evidence" and "research." I listen to the words the person I'm trying to influence uses and go from there.

> **Example:** "James, you told me you have faith in God's plan. He wouldn't have put us in the same room for no

MANIPULATION AND DARK PSYCHOLOGY

reason." or "Sam, there is no proof that James took your sandwich but there are crumbs at his desk."

Disagree On Some Things: Nobody believes someone that only agrees with us.

Sharing an opposing viewpoint or two is a normal part of an honest and persuasive conversation. No proposal is perfect and having a small difference allows me to show how I mitigate and overcome problems. This provides me with an early goodwill for later disagreements that might be bigger.

The people I need to convince understand that we can't agree on *everything*. By giving them something small and easily overcome, they assume every conflict will be as easy to resolve. This makes them easier to persuade because they know that I understand and can work with their misgivings.

> **Example:** "Let me stop you there, Jim. I agree that reduced taxes are good for all citizens, but the top 1% benefit more than the rest of us. So are you going to keep letting them get the benefits while you labor here in the mud, or are you going to join the big dogs and sign the document?"

Draw Positive Conclusions: Get better at influencing others.

If the goal is to produce change, focus on encouraging and directing that change. I give the people I am trying to influence the direction I want them to go. It starts them on the track I want and makes it harder for them to argue with me because their mind is already primed.

It takes more mental effort to come up with a new option than to accept and go along with an already established one. Take them where they need to be, not somewhere they need to avoid.

> **Example:** "You like walking right? Do you want to be able to walk your daughter down the aisle on her wedding day? So tell me the combination to the safe and you get to keep both of your kneecaps."

Choose the Right Medium: Some things are harder in person.

There is a big reason why every job requires a résumé before an interview. Face-to-face interactions allow emotions to cloud decisions in a way that text, video, and audio doesn't, so I avoid using them first if I need the person I'm influencing to avoid being emotional.

If I have a choice, I always email people I don't know well before meeting them. Especially if the meeting is about a business offer or suggestion. But I make it a point to see friends and loved ones in person before asking favors or offering advice.

Always Be Right: Every structure needs a skeleton.

Arguments are built on foundations of language and logic. Framing is almost as important as delivery, but the best way to be persuasive, to begin with, is to have the right message.

The most effective persuaders make sure the message is framed and delivered in a way that matters. Effective speakers are clear, concise, and to the point. They succeed because of sound data, reasoning, and irreproachable conclusions. Thus, I make sure I have something to back me up before I start influencing anyone.

Chapter 2: Neuro-Linguistic Programming

Neuro-linguistic programming (NLP) is an approach to communication, personal development, and psychotherapy created by Richard Bandler and John Grinder in California in the 1970s that leverages the power of language to influence thought.

NLP has infiltrated every element of modern business life. *Everyone* in sales or marketing has practiced these methods to some degree, but psychoanalysts and occult leaders around the world give it a bad name.

Most people don't grasp the underlying principles and struggle to apply them in everyday environments.

But some skilled individuals can harness this power to give them an unbeatable advantage. The techniques are best used in a one-on-one or small group environment. The fewer people involved, the easier it is to read and apply NLP methods.

NLP is a complex subject and is often taught over the course of years. That's because it takes practice to learn the range of reactions people can express. But the promise of learning people's inner secrets makes this technique especially attractive to con artists and law enforcement.

NLP is basically a method of reading a person to understand their personality and individual quirks. NLP users watch for subtle cues that are invisible to most people and use them to control a conversation and the emotions of the people in it. Eye movement, skin flush, pupil dilation, and nervous tics all provide information.

After an initial round of observation, skilled users can mimic their subject in subtle but impactful ways. The NLP user thus opens their target to suggestion and steers them toward an intended destination.

A skilled NLP user can determine:

Which side of the brain their subject uses

People fall along a spectrum between creative and analytical. New science shows that brain function is actually distributed across the brain. But it is still helpful to think of people through this lens.

Word choice, sentence structure, and associations all reveal details about the person that uses them. I begin by looking at what my target is saying and how they present their points, then I adjust my words to be more analytical or emotional based on my subject.

Left-brained people often use words that elicit emotion or

experiences. Right-brained people like to include things outside their experience or expertise.

> **Example:** Left-brained people: "That looks fun. I bet we can squeeze in!" Right-brained people: "Is that safe? Is it rated for someone my size?"

Which sense is most important to them

We have more than the five senses (sight, sound, taste, touch, and smell) most people know about. We also have a sense of order, balance, morality and a host of others, and each of us has one or two that are more important than the rest.

I listen to see which sense is most important to my target. Then I use some of the same words they did in my reply.

> **Example:** If vision is important to my subject, I say things like, "Do you see what I'm saying?" Audio-focused people respond better to "Can you hear where I'm coming from?" Meanwhile, I might ask a taste-oriented individual to "savor that for a moment."

How their brain stores information.

Our brains are the most complex computers we have ever come across. They store and process billions of bits of information a second. Each one functions a little differently. One of the biggest areas of divergence is in how people store information.

Some individuals have a memory like a sponge, soaking up

everything near them. Others are more like a strainer that catches big chunks and allows everything to pass through. NLP techniques help people discern the difference and to what degree.

Over time, NLP users get better at keeping track of information. With enough time, users can improve their information tracking abilities to near-genius levels. This gives us an advantage over anyone who isn't as experienced or naturally gifted.

I use this information to determine how much info I need to overwhelm my subject. If I want to lose them in the details, I simply include more than they can keep straight. If I want them to follow along, I keep the details and figures to a minimum.

> **Example:** I will occasionally remember something wrong on purpose. It's best with something small like a phone number or address. If my subject corrects me, I can see how well they store information. The average person can only hold seven numbers in their head at once so it normally only takes me asking for them to remember two phone numbers to see where they fall along the spectrum.

When they are lying or making things up.

People perform specific behaviors when they make things up called "tells." NLP users like me can pick up on these tells and be able to call out the liar as they lie. Some people are better than others at lying but everyone has at least one tell.

Skilled liars understand that for someone else to believe their lie, so must they. So they convince themselves of it first. They often don't display all the signs of dishonesty because they truly believe the lie as they tell it.

Practice can help people fall for their own lie but the process demands a selective memory. This feature is more reliably detected than the oft-cited slight downward glance. It also proves to be a more consistent indicator of ingrained deception than awkward looks. Power imbalances also make a refusal to make eye contact less reliable as well.

> **Example:** When my best friend (let's call him Ted) won't look me in the eye during his story. He keeps looking down and to one side of me, then the other. Another person (let's call him Fred) tells his story without looking away at all.
>
> When Ted looks away I become suspicious, but Fred's refusal to look away is also a red flag. If they are subjects, I cut them some slack. As long as they don't change demeanor mid-story I can attribute some of it to simple nervousness.

How to make someone drop their guard.

NLP users like myself leverage these techniques to convince

others that I am just like them. People can't help but like someone they recognize as a kindred spirit. So I combine the techniques above to highlight our similarities.

The more alike we are, the more a subject likes me. So I listen intently to what they are saying. Then I respond to them with the signals that I know appeal to their inner selves. This encourages my subjects to reveal more about themselves to me willingly.

When someone likes you, they want to include you in their lives. Listening to what they say often provides deep insight into what controls their lives. People offer up their darkest secrets willingly, believing that I truly understand them.

So you can condition people without their consent/knowledge.

Let's face it, people don't like finding out someone was manipulating them. It violates the idea that we are in control of our lives. But sometimes the truth is hard to take, and we need someone to help us see the way without calling us out on it.

We all manipulate those around us to one degree or another. This can be as simple as breaking a bad habit or establishing new relationship rules with a toxic family member. By steering them in the right direction, we can help them respond how we prefer.

NLP doesn't brainwash someone (that's covered elsewhere) or cause them to do something out of character. But it does reveal the strings that control each of us. What you do with those strings once you have them is up to you.

Once the subjects are open and receptive, I present my request in terms that they would prefer. I use strong action words with leaders, comforting and kind words with emotionally sensitive subjects, and common words with the less educated. I do everything in my power to appear similar to my subject in thought and deed. This ensures they are the most receptive to my desires and avoids having to issue orders and ultimatums.

Example: When I need a favor, I never ask for it right out the gate. Instead, I begin by building rapport. I ensure my body language is open and tailor my questions and responses to the person I am trying to influence.

Chapter 3: Cognitive Behavioral Therapy

Cognitive behavioral therapy (CBT) is a type of psychotherapeutic treatment that helps patients understand the thoughts and feelings that influence behaviors. CBT is commonly used to treat a wide range of disorders, including phobias, addictions, depression, and anxiety, but it can also stimulate them.

Indications are clear that the majority of phobias develop in early childhood. As people grow into teenagers and then adults, they are less likely to develop new phobias. By around 30-35, most people stop developing new fears.

Children can easily develop the same phobias as their parents if they become progressively more aware of it. These phobias are the hardest to overcome during adult life. Once I become aware of your specific phobias, I can use that knowledge to control and manipulate people.

But not all fears and phobias are the same. Some are simple and elemental while others are esoteric and multilayered. Knowing how to induce or repress these fears allows me to control myself and others.

Causes for Simple Phobias: Simple phobias are specific fears that often develop in early childhood between 4 and 8 years old. Traumatic and unpleasant experiences can plant a seed of fear. If that seed is nurtured over enough time, it will eventually grow into a phobia.

Experiments show that there is little to no genetic element to phobias. Parents can't pass on fears in the same way they pass on hair color, but a phobia can be learned from a parent as the child grows.

> **Example:** If a parent has arachnophobia (the fear of spiders) when their child is born, their child is more likely develop the same or similar phobia than not. The parent's behavior can pass on the fear because the child is hyper-aware of it growing up.

Causes for Complex Phobias: Unlike simple versions, complex phobias are complicated and shrouded in mystery and ambiguity. These phobias are created by combining life experiences, brain chemistry, and genetics. Stressful situations are a more common instigator of social phobias than physiological problems like agoraphobia.

Complex phobias are part of our evolutionary history. The instincts that cause someone to obsess over their social media profile are the same ones that keep a small tribe together during a famine. Avoiding wide open spaces can lower the risk of dangerous predators like lions in the past. It can also lead someone to feel safer indoors than outside.

There is also a biochemical element to complex phobias.

Neuroscience shows us that people use their whole brain, not just 10% like the movies always claim. But the functions of thought are spread across different structures.

Memories are processed in a different area of the brain than the part that controls digestion and heart rate. The amygdala is one of the oldest parts of the brain and bypasses all the logic structures by controlling our fight or flight reflexes among other functions. It can be chemically triggered to reinforce a specific emotion (most often fear) with whatever stimuli are present.

This means that you can effectively replace one emotion connected to a memory or person with another. Because the part that stores information about dangerous events and deadly threats can be made to trigger with any memory, it's easy to induce a phobia if you don't care about the target.

If I want a target afraid of bunnies, repeatedly triggering their amygdala around bunnies will eventually induce a phobia of bunnies. I can use the same technique to cause a phobia of phones, sexual acts, and almost anything else. This is a common technique used in conversion therapy because of its effectiveness in a controlled environment. But it does suffer from some drawbacks.

The effects can be reversed by similar methods showing that there is nothing to fear. Negative reinforcement is more effective though so it normally takes longer to recover from the induced phobia than it took to instill it.

Example: By ensuring that pain comes every time a subject sees a specific symbol, I can trigger the targets amygdala. Once the association is established, putting the symbol on a door will ensure they avoid going near it unless otherwise compelled. By creating the simple phobia of a symbol, I can establish a complex phobia of specific places or people.

Causes of Addiction

Drug addiction has plagued civilization for as long as we have records. But it is also a major factor in compromising cognitive behavior. Prolonged exposure to certain substances produces a compulsive craving, seeking, and use that persists in the face of severe consequences.

Drug addiction works by stimulating the reward pathways of the brain located in the nucleus accumbens and the prefrontal cortex. These pathways process pleasure and are easy to damage. Some drugs interact with these pathways in ways that lend themselves to manipulation.

When cocaine is smoked, snorted or injected, it travels through the bloodstream to the brain. Although it hits the whole brain, it mainly interacts with the reward pathways to create a euphoric effect. This effect comes from neurotransmitters releasing like dopamine releasing faster than normal.

Unfortunately for longtime users, neurotransmitters like

dopamine get produced at a set rate. So it takes progressively more to produce the same effect. This is called a drug resistance and is one of the major contributors to overdoses as people chase the first time.

Drug dealers come to power by securing themselves as the sole source of the chemicals their customers/victims demand. They leverage the chemical dependence created by substances like cocaine and methamphetamine to control their subjects and extract everything of value they can. Threats to their supply often result in addicts resorting to desperate behavior.

Be careful when relying on addiction to control cognitive behavior. Subjects are beholden to their addiction first, your will second. As soon as your target finds an alternative source, they are likely to switch allegiance if they don't have other reasons to remain loyal.

> **Example:** If I want to gain control over an addict, I first must control their supply. Drugs, alcohol, gambling and sex addiction all work in a similar way. Once in control, I can reduce their access when they don't do what I want and increase it when they do. The longer I maintain their dependence, the stronger their need for it and the more reliable my control.

Benefit From Addiction

Whether you use them or not, illegal drugs are big business.

Americans spend almost a trillion dollars getting high on illegal drugs every year. With so much money going around, most drug markets are flooded with competition.

In addition to having lots of competition, most drug users have access to highly potent products. The science behind drugs like acid, heroin, and cocaine means that it's easy for competitors to match product quality. Even drugs with a wide range of raw forms (like marijuana) are easily refined to a given concentration.

So intrepid capitalists need to do something to stand out from all the other drug dealers. Cartels have to find novel ways to advertise their products if they want to get ahead. In effect, making money dealing drugs is all about advertising.

There will always be the die-hards who will consume anything that crosses their path. But a clever marketing campaign or gimmick can make or break a spontaneous sale. But not all marketing ploys are created equal.

There is a real art to coming up with compelling marketing, but once you figure out what works, the sky is the limit. I've put together some real-world examples of marketing gimmicks that helped dealers stand out and profit.

Drug Survival Kit: Music festivals and other big events are a prime place for selling and consuming drugs. Many festival-goers struggle to find all the supplies they need and are willing to pay a premium for an all-inclusive kit.

Different drugs have unique paraphernalia needed for consumption. All that gear needs to be carried around as well. But it also needs to be discreet enough to pass security and cursory police inspections.

The more compact and discrete these kits are, the better. They don't need to have much of the actual drug, either. Include a small to medium dose of whatever substance chosen to limit the time it takes someone to come back for more.

> **Example:** A marijuana drug survival kit includes the following: a lighter or other sources of flame; a glass pipe, rolling papers, or vape pen; about one gram of marijuana; and a container to hold it all. Adding things like chewing gum, a water bottle, and breath mints are cost-effective ways to entice people to go for the kit.

Name Brand: Name brands lend authority to the products and services they endorse. People will often prefer an item with a familiar brand over a novel one, even if they are the same product. Tapping into the association of a person allows advertisers of any product to create a cognitive bias in favor of their offer.

We are conditioned to associate certain brands and images with feelings or emotions and repel others. This makes it important to think about what brands the customer already buys. The more familiar the brand, the more inclined a subject is to choose it with everything else being the same.

Brands like Chanel, Armani, and Mercedes attract a different demographic than Winchester, Smith & Wesson, and Glock. There is some brand overlap in niche populations but if the target isn't a member of them, it might repel them instead of enticing. Make sure to adjust the brand to the intended target and venue for best results.

> **Example:** If I want to sell a product to a woman at a club, I might label it with Chanel, but if I am selling to a man getting ready for hunting season, I might paint the container with Realtree camo. Both ways I am able to charge a premium without changing the actual quality of the product.

Buy Two, Get One Free: Higher quality products often get away with higher prices. People expect to pay more when they get more. We will often pay more than the minimum if we think it is a better value.

By offering a reward after reaching a certain limit, I encourage people to at least hit that limit. If I structure it properly, I can offset the cost of the promotion with the increased price. The incentive makes people feel like they are getting a better deal when each person actually spends more money overall.

> **Example:** I can make someone fear they are missing out by offering a better deal once they reach some additional marker. Since everybody wants the best deal possible, they are significantly more likely to try

reaching that new goal to keep from missing out on the better deal. At the end of the day, they get more than they needed/wanted and I get more money in my pocket than if I had only sold one.

Offer A Rainbow: We love feeling individual and getting to show others how unique we are. It is a fundamental part of establishing and maintaining an identity. It makes sense that we gravitate to activities and items that reflect the best parts of ourselves.

People crave the ability to stand out. By offering multiple options, it shifts their focus from asking "if they should buy" to "what to buy". Even though there isn't any difference in the actual product, the perceived difference makes it stand out and sell better.

There is such thing as too many choices. Having too many options leads to decision paralysis as the mind struggles to sort them out, so keep the number of options below seven to ensure maximum returns.

> **Example:** If I want to make an impression at a Pride parade or similar event, I offer different-colored options of the same item. I include the whole spectrum and people love getting to pick out their favorite color of whatever I'm selling. The "personalized" versions almost always sell out faster than the "generic" goods and services.

31

Chapter 4: Social Manipulation

Social manipulation occurs when a person's emotions, opinions, or behaviors are affected by others. Social influence takes many forms and can be seen in conformity, socialization, peer pressure, obedience, leadership, persuasion, sales, and marketing.

We can't have a conversation about social manipulation without talking about Stanley Milgram and his experiments. That's because the techniques Mr. Milgram used are brutally effective and repeatable. They also have terrifying implications about authority and acts of evil.

The Milgram Experiment

> **Primary Question:** How far will someone go to obey an authority figure, even when ordered to act against their moral conscience?

> **Methods:** Volunteers were asked to "teach" other people to improve their ability to remember. A man in a white coat posing as a doctor asked the volunteer teacher to administer questions to a "learner" in another room within earshot. If the learner answered incorrectly, the teacher was directed to provide an electric shock.

> The idea was that for every wrong answer, the shock

would teach them to not answer incorrectly. After every mistake, the doctor directed the teacher to increase the voltage delivered to the learner. The control panel presented to the teacher included settings in 10-volt increments up to a lethal 450 volts.

If a teacher protested and asked to stop, the doctor would reply "The experiment must go on." Any protests or questions from the teachers would be answered with the same words. The doctors were not otherwise allowed to coerce and were strictly forbidden from forcing them to do anything.

An actor played the learner in the other room and would scream, wail, plead and beg for the teacher to stop before finally going silent. It's important that the teacher not see the learner during the experiment or the success rate drops. The learners can scream and plea all they want.

Results: In one example, about 90% of teachers delivered a lethal shock before stopping. Only about 1% of the population was willing to go all the way to the maximum shock without coercion. But despite teachers voicing protests to the doctor, they continued to conduct the test. Often teachers continued to deliver fatal shocks long after the learner stopped replying to prompts.

Even though having a form of authority is a major contributor to success at social manipulation, it's not foolproof. You have to leverage that authority properly to produce the best results. There are twelve strategies to accomplish this task in a minimum amount of time.

Sow the Seeds of Fear

Fear is one of the most powerful emotions. It captures our attention like nothing else, threatening everything we hold dear. It forces us to focus on it and shuts down our higher thinking.

It doesn't matter that violence is on a global centuries-long decline. It's easy to manufacture situations that make it seem like extreme violence is the norm. Just hone in on the frightening but statistical rarities.

Terrorist attacks and mass shootings might be rare compared to lightning strikes and police killings but are terrifying enough to shut down our creative thinking skills and force us to focus on defending ourselves. This fear is then easily translated into fear at whatever scapegoat is convenient.

> **Example:** Major news networks understand the power of fear. They offer 24-hour coverage of all the things going wrong in the world. They offer a warped view because they prioritize content that produces a strong emotional reaction to an accurate representation of the facts.

34

Provoke Anger and Hostility

Many creatures naturally respond to fear with anger and aggression. When you are a mouse cornered by a cat, it makes sense to go on the offensive. In such situations, the risk of dying is outweighed by the chance of escape. This dichotomy is often referred to as the fight or flight response.

There are tons of times when our fear is justified, but we can set up false dichotomies in our every-day life that make us feel like a trapped mouse when we really aren't. Mass media makes its bread and butter off setting up and playing up any threat they can.

The bigger and more complex the issue, the more anger and hostility it generates. Offering a simple solution might never fix the problem but most people prefer doing something, even if it makes things worse. If it does exacerbate the situation, it is easy to blame the increased tension on the complex and intractable problem.

> **Example:** Provoking hostility and rage is a simple matter when you know what people are afraid of. That's why politicians are so good at stoking up fervor in their supporters. They identify the fears of their constituents, blame scapegoats and offer simple answers to intractable solutions.

Play a Messiah Figure

There have been a lot of people who claimed to be the only

person that can do what needs to be done. These people are almost always dominant and strong-willed. They offer domination and don't think twice about making unrealistic claims.

The best way to become a messiah is by leveraging the afterlife. This doesn't always mean religion though. Many dictators present themselves as the only person capable of bringing back a mythical golden age.

This strategy leverages nostalgia and totalitarian security to alleviate a social fear. It relies on the promise of better things to come in order to justify whatever the Great Leader desires. This makes it more effective with conservative populations than liberal ones.

> **Example:** To gain control over a group, I would claim to be the only person who can "Make Things Great Again." I position myself as the sole authority willing to do what needs to be done. This forces anyone in the group to remain silent on issues they might disagree on. The silence acts as a form of de facto consent, which prevents others from speaking up, in fear of being the only one to go against the Great Leader.

Paint in Black and White

The world is supremely complex and there are many ways to accomplish any given goal. But this idea doesn't make people feel very secure, so we have a tendency to try and simplify things.

Simplifying complex problems normally isn't an issue. But when all possible responses are reduced to two options, it can set up a false and misleading dilemma. This warped view of things makes it easy to justify all sorts of bad behavior.

Reducing the world to black-and-white narratives appeals to our desire for simple and clean resolutions to complex and messy problems. It becomes more effective when we are on the brink of catastrophe. When people are afraid and angry, they often accept these oversimplifications and alluring but empty promises.

> **Example:** When I want to polarize a group, I introduce a "with us or against us" mentality. By making every issue an all-or-nothing debate, I force my opponents to fight everything I stand for, even if they don't disagree on everything. People either believe me and support everything I stand for or are seen as a threat trying to undermine my followers.

Deflect with Humor

There is always a chance that an enemy can get the better of you, but letting people see that can ruin any attempts to establish yourself as a strongman or messiah. One method to hide an obvious foil is to deflect the blow with cutting humor.

Laughter disrupts traditional patterns of speech. It's hard to stay mad at someone who makes you laugh uncontrollably. A properly timed joke makes you laugh and be more receptive to the next thing said.

> **Example:** When I notice I am losing control of a situation, a touch of humor can get me back in the driver seat. If my opponent is focusing on my small following, I can often shut them down instantly by making a joke about how few people follow them. If delivered properly, it derails their attack and puts them on the defensive.

Act Superior to Opponents

The more respect you show to opponents, the more powerful they appear. Responding with disbelief and disgust informs everyone that I don't believe the topic or critique is worthy of my time. It also puts pressure on the person delivering the attack to show why I need to take them seriously.

This can bypass all sorts of rational discussion and produce a win despite damning assertions by my opponent. It makes them look confused and insecure when their main point of contention is dismissed as a fool's banter. They then need to take time and energy to show why their point is valid instead of continuing their attack.

> **Example:** If I want to dismiss a critic, I treat their questions and assertions with disbelief and disgust. I go

out of my way to show that the attack is ridiculous, laughable, and not even worthy of attention. I tailor my responses to show how foolish the critique is and request "real" or "grown-up" perspectives.

Make It About You

Whether making jokes or acting superior, I always aim to appear as the leader of a game others simply play. This is accomplished by framing every interaction as if I am the best there is. But it takes a strong and unflinching frame to really sell.

Staying at the center of any debate is essential to manipulate the crowd. You need them to care about your thoughts and opinions, not those of an opponent. Once your frame is established, make sure others can't challenge it directly.

Combining power plays with some of the other tactics like provoking anger and presenting myself as the best thing since bread creates a difficult combination to counter. The more manipulative elements I can combine, the more untouchable, iron-willed and courageous I appear.

Example: When giving a speech, I lead with a little fear-mongering, stoking the flames of anger towards an intractable problem and weathering the storm with a little humor. Then when the crowd is properly riled up, I tell them how I can help them overcome the Big Bad

Problem controlling their life. I explain how my experience and innate understanding helps me find solutions to problems. Throughout it all, I make sure my talking points and I stay the focus.

Create Double-Bind Situations

Another tactic that improves frame control is to trap an opponent is a situation where it doesn't matter how they respond. I ask questions and make statements that put others in a lose-lose situation. Any response makes me look better and make them look worse.

The goal of this method is to discredit and steamroll opponents. If they rise to the challenge, it looks like they are simply reacting to your jabs. But if they do nothing, they appear weak and scared.

> **Example:** When in a debate, I might say "I see that my opponent is trying to build his energy, but it's not working." If they increase energy, it looks like I'm in control, but maintaining/lowering their energy sets them up to be steamrolled later in the debate.

Repeat, Repeat, Repeat

Our brains are hard-wired to recognize patterns and give them meaning. The more times we see or hear something, the more likely we are to believe it's true. If nothing around us contradicts the pattern, then this is even truer.

We find comfort in patterns and complete sets, so much so that we are often compelled to complete known patterns. So companies and people set up patterns of behavior and thought that take advantage of this principle.

It takes a lot of repetition for something to stick in your mind. That's one reason companies pour billions of dollars into ads to win your dollars. They understand that hearing something enough times will make you start to believe it, even if you know it's a lie.

Repeating emotionally provocative words like "winning" or short and repetitive phrases help them sink into the listeners. This tactic subtly conditions people to associate the word and the subject because of how often they appear together. Company jingles and ad campaigns leverage this phenomenon to sell more products or convince you to buy things you don't need.

> **Example:** Dairy farmers managed to increase milk sales significantly with their "Got Milk?" campaign. Recording and political companies also leverage repetition to encourage consumption of their media. Fast food companies also use catchy jingles across media platforms to overwhelm listeners and get "I'm lovin' it," "I want my baby back, baby back," and "How many licks does it take" stuck in your head decades after the campaign ends.

Use Social Proof

Humans are social creatures with certain perverse tendencies. One of those is that we tend to do and believe whatever we think everyone else does. That's why effective social manipulators always seem to have the back of the majority.

It doesn't mean the majority actually supports them, though. Social proof is easy to manufacture with a small minority and the right study or poll. But as long as there is the perception of support, it's hard to argue.

> **Example:** "Nobody believes you are a serious candidate, Bill. In fact, the latest polls show I'm ahead by double digits. Everybody can tell your ship has sunk."

Appeal to Authority

In our modern day and age, there is too much information for normal people to process. They are flooded with competing ideas and facts from every angle, so everyone tends to use experts' inputs to form their opinions.

Experts don't have to be highly qualified, though. They only need the mantle of authority placed on them. This can authority be anything from a title like Brain Surgeon to heading a faction like President of the WWO.

This means that high-status individuals create a stronger likelihood of a subject agreeing with a conclusion that is obviously fake. The appeal to authority is often able to apply enough pressure to force conformity from the majority.

> **Example:** "My opponent was investigated by the FBI, CIA, and NSA last year. Only someone with something to hide would have so many agencies looking into their past."

Appeal to Irrational Parts of the Brain

Humans are emotion-driven, irrational monsters of the natural world. Despite our best wishes, emotions, and feelings drive our actions far more than logic and reason. That's okay most of the time because they often indicate an appropriate course of action.

But then there are times when our emotions betray us or at least serve our goals poorly. Without training to identify and overcome the natural cognitive bias we all hold, our emotions open us up to most of the techniques covered so far.

Even people trained to identify and overcome the irrational parts of the brain struggle to resist. These individuals appear resistant but are as weak to social manipulation as anyone else. They just require a more adept and skilled hand.

> **Example:** The more authority you have over a person, the more you can force them to your will. If I assume the mantle of authority, I get to give the commands and determine the morals of the group. Religions, charity,

and clubs all offer local control over a group of people expecting to follow the leader's will. Once in a position of authority, you can slowly turn up the voltage of your demands. Try to limit your target's access to alternative sources of authority. Never let them forget that they can't trust other sources of information.

Chapter 5: Subliminal Messaging

A subliminal message is a signal or message designed to pass below (sub) the normal limits of perception. For example, it might be inaudible to the conscious mind (but audible to the unconscious or deeper mind) or might be an image transmitted briefly and unperceived consciously and yet perceived unconsciously.

People have been using subliminal messages to influence thought since at least the Greeks back in 500 B.C. They employed a method called *rhetoric*. Rhetoric is a carefully chosen language the speaker uses to persuade or impress listeners.

The idea behind this ancient form of mind control is that the words and images we see or hear influence the way we think. Describing a place as a dump conjures a different image and feeling than calling it a palace. By choosing specific words to describe an idea or person, they could influence the opinion of that character without directly stating it.

This method of control became popular with thinkers, politicians, and poets who continue to use it to this day. Blockbuster films and television series employ these methods with scientific precision. Unfortunately, the audience often views the message as fake or insincere.

There is a lot of diversity in the world. What inflames one person to hate might not cause any reaction in another. That hasn't stopped people from trying to control others with words. Our world is full of hundreds of countries with thousands of dialects because of the ongoing war of words and the struggle to control their meaning.

But we are more alike than we are different. Humans tend to fall into general thought patterns, regardless of national origin or political ideology. Using the right words at the right time can persuade someone to unwittingly believe something they wouldn't otherwise.

Over the last 2,500 years, the use of rhetoric and iconography to condition thought has grown more complex. Religious buildings and shrines really embraced the idea that images can convey meaning during the middle ages. By the 20th century, people understood that we respond to many stimuli without even noticing them.

Subliminal messages are signals that pass below the normal limits of perception. They can be transmitted briefly and are unconsciously registered. These signals contain information that works to control certain conscious decisions.

This type of mind control was the holy grail of business and military after World War 2. The chance to control someone without them even realizing it seemed like a fever dream. But it didn't take long for researchers to work out the specifics of how it works.

In 1957 a market researcher named James Vicary came up with the idea of inserting words into a movie. He chose to study the effectiveness of using the words "Eat Popcorn" and "Drink Coca-Cola". So he inserted a single frame of each phrase at strategic points in the feature.

After reporting overwhelming success, marketers around the world started getting in on the action. But businesses weren't the only people looking to control people. The American and Russian militaries were very interested in subliminal messaging during the Cold War.

The two superpowers poured untold amounts of money into researching the effectiveness of subliminal messages and other forms of mind control. Their experiments went undetected for years before their cover was blown. Despite many setbacks, the research helped establish the methods and test the reliability of subliminal messages.

It was eventually revealed that Vicary made up his movie theater results. But that didn't stop business and government researchers. They continued trying to hammer out the details of how and when subliminal messaging works.

There are three general types of subliminal message. Each works in a different way to achieve the same result. These messages often include a sexual element in an attempt to bypass the logical centers of the brain.

Subvisual Messages: These are visual cues that are flashed too quickly to register. This type also includes images that can be viewed multiple ways. Ones in movies and TV can be displayed anywhere from one to a few hundred milliseconds. A single frame of a movie is about the outside limit of this methods effective range. But they simply need to go unnoticed in print or still images.

These messages are easy to identify because they often exist as a still image or other concrete media. Print ads in magazines and newspapers are full of subvisual images. Most are sexual in nature, although there are religious and economic ideologies in there as well.

> **Example:** Cigarette companies, Disney animators, and alcohol producers use subvisual messages constantly. From the shape of King Triton's palace to the color of smokers in Phillip Morris adverts, subvisual images are everywhere.

Subaudible Messages: These are audio cues that are inserted into louder audio sources like music or narration. They rely on the power of the overlying audio to keep them from being detected. The longer someone listens to this type of message, the more effective it is supposed to be.

The United States Military experimented with this technique extensively during the 1950's and 1960's but eventually abandoned the technique. They concluded that it was ineffective at best and operationally useless at worst.

> **Example:** This technique is common for self-help courses and other empowerment products. It was also used during Project MK Ultra by the CIA where they paid doctors to help erase memories. The effects were no better than a placebo so it was relegated to late night infomercials.

Backmasking: These are audio messages that are recorded backward. By playing them normally, the messages sound innocuous. Played in reverse, the message becomes clear. There is no duration component beyond needing to hear the entire message.

This technique only became possible after the invention and widespread use of tape recording software. It caught on quickly in the music industry as many contemporary artists experimented with new recording techniques. Fundamentalist Christians eventually latched on to this idea during the late 1970's and early 1980s.

Allegations of Satanic backmasking began cropping up in the early 1980s. Christian lecturers warned of the dangers of these hidden messages from Satan in popular music. Their claims that Satan inspired Led Zeppelin to write "Stairway to Heaven" along with other musicians continues to this day.

But religious zealots aren't the only people that believe in the power of this technique. The religious fervor sparked curiosity in government officials and military personnel. Their research only showed that it has minimal effect and couldn't find any evidence of demonic possession.

> **Example:** The Beatles incorporated backmasking into their 1966 album *Revolver*. The songs "Tomorrow Never Knows," "I'm Only Sleeping," and "Rain" all included backmasking techniques. The Beatles became the center of controversy over the technique after Paul McCartney died and listeners discovered the words "Paul is a dead man, miss him, miss him, miss him" in *I'm So Tired.*

After decades of research and untold billions invested, there didn't seem to be a limit on the reach of subliminal messages, but it did show some major weaknesses and limits in its application. By its very nature, subliminal messages have minimal impact on actual behavior.

Subtle changes below the level of conscious perception have subtle effects. They are powerful tools for directing thought but often fail to make a noticeable impact. If the subject doesn't have the right motivation, it might not work at all.

Some brain imaging studies show that we respond to

subliminal messages in measurable ways. Activity levels change in the emotion-processing center of the brain, called the amygdala. Changes are also visible in the insula, hippocampus, and visual cortex, which control awareness, memories, and vision respectively.

This technique doesn't implant thoughts and actions into the subjects head. Instead, it guides or directs thoughts and actions in a specific direction. This severely limits the effectiveness of subliminal messages.

People Must Have a Need: For subliminal messages to work, the target needs to already want to do the behavior. This limits the overall reach of this technique but still allows for plenty of versatility. I just need to target a need they might not know they have.

If push comes to shove, I can engineer a stimulus to trigger the need I want to exploit. This is a common practice in the beauty and diamond markets. They engineer a need for their product (to attract sexual partners or retain them) and then offer their service to fulfill this need. It doesn't matter that the product is a placebo, the people end up buying the promise because deep down they want to.

There will always be someone who refuses to buy-in to an idea. Individuals adverse to or uninterested in the stimuli might actually be repelled by an effective subliminal message. But the more the subject already desires a good or service, the more influential the message.

Example: Researchers found that study participants flashed with images of a brand name drink were more likely to choose that brand later. The effect was statistically significant and reinforced the idea that subliminal messages work.

There were limitations to how much influence it had. The effect was limited in scope and was effective only on people already primed for the product. They also found some participants didn't change their preferences if they had a strong aversion to the brand.

Chapter 6: Psychological Warfare

Psychological warfare is a type of social influence that aims to change the behavior or perception of others through abusive, deceptive, or underhanded tactics.

The term "psychological warfare" is broad enough to be difficult to nail down. But it essentially boils down to a type of social influence that aims to change the perception of others. Often this is done to reduce an opponent's morale or mental stability.

One of the most infamous examples of psychological warfare techniques is called the MK Ultra project. This secret program by American intelligence agencies used unwilling participants from vulnerable populations during the 1950-60s. The goal was to discover a way to control whole populations without their knowledge.

The MK Ultra project experimented extensively with pharmacological control techniques. This included dozens of substances including marijuana, cocaine, and lysergic acid diethylamide (LSD). LSD became the focus of their experiments early on and was used on people without their knowledge.

By experimenting on the civilian population without informing them, they were able to study the effects in real-world situations. Once the project became public knowledge over 20 years later, dozens of unsuspecting victims were dead. An unknown number of others were permanently harmed in the course of the experiments.

A scientist named Frank Olson worked for the CIA in 1953 when they took him to a retreat. They then dosed him with LSD in a cocktail without his knowledge. He became the first person we know of to die from the experiments.

Olson died a few days later when he threw himself from a New York City hotel room on November 28, 1953. His death was originally ruled suicide but the victim's family decided to have a second autopsy in 1994. A team of forensic experts discovered multiple injuries that seemed to have happened before the fall.

The findings sparked controversy over CIA activities and public outrage. The family was eventually awarded $750,000 and a personal apology from President Gerald Ford and CIA Director William Colby. But Olson didn't have it as rough as some of the MK Ultra victims.

Mental patients were some of the worst treated of the test subjects. Government sanctioned doctors eventually used certain interrogation techniques developed with these drugs. Often, the victims never fully recovered from the effects of the event.

LSD inhibits the brain from working properly, opening people up to suggestion. It was used to prepare the victim for an interrogation. Injection resulted in a faster onset than other methods.

Once the person was tripping from a large dose, the interrogator would begin questioning in a variety of ways. These techniques are forbidden in normal science as they are cruel and unusual. Performing them is as likely to get you behind bars as anything else and are some of the cruelest forms of psychological warfare.

Sensory Deprivation: This technique involves long periods without physical or mental stimulation. It can be achieved through drug-induced sleep periods or special chambers along with electric shocks.

The first method involves drug-induced sleep periods. At the same time, the patient needs intravenous nutrition during the treatment. The result of prolonged periods of this technique is induced amnesia.

With enough nutrition supplementation, a victim can remain unconscious for months. One patient was kept asleep for 65 days. Victims had amnesia for up to six months after the end of the treatment.

Similar effects come from using sensory deprivation chambers. These lightless chambers are filled with saltwater (for buoyancy) at skin temperature. Sound dampening ensures that people within cannot see, hear or feel anything.

This technique allows for people to have new backgrounds suggested to them. Emotional conflicts can be induced as easily as anything else, but it also suffers from unreliability.

Depatterning: This technique attempts to break up patterns of behavior. To achieve this, they started prolonged sleep with multiple shock therapy six times higher than normal. Some LSD was added to the mix at the end of each shock session and audio tapes are played during the sleep cycles.

This cycle was repeated for up to 81 days in one case. The victim experienced complete amnesia and never recovered her memories. She had to go through mental and physical therapy to regain basic functions like walking and talking.

Unfortunately, this method is no more effective than less drastic methods. It also leaves permanent mental damage. When people find out about it, there is significant blowback, making it a dangerous method for even the evilest person.

Don't Forget Propaganda: Propaganda plays a large role in effective psychological warfare against communities. It leverages fear, uncertainty, and terror to coerce groups of people into making mistakes. The best part is that it accomplishes this without using physical force.

We don't always need to wage war with military troops. In

addition to being costly, military action always has a chance of failure. It is often better to sap the will of enemies and avoid physical confrontations.

Propaganda is able to sap the will to fight and sew dissension in the ranks. It encourages strife or infighting among enemies, or it can subdue or calm outraged sections of society. That's why companies and governments engage with it at every possible opportunity.

There are six main ways to utilize propaganda for psychological warfare. Each method hits a different part of the population and has different requirements. Combining as many of the techniques listed below leads to a most operational success.

News Outlets: Most people get information about the world from the news. It might be a local evening news station, a cable show, or on the internet. Luckily, most of these sources are controlled by a small group of people.

Billionaire Amazon founder Jeff Bezos purchased the Washington Post. This old-school news source reaches millions of people a month and holds a power of authority far beyond anything Bezos could create himself. Using this news source, he is able to ensure his perspective is presented by the network.

Rupert Murdock of News Corp. created an international network instead of just buying one newspaper. One of the most influential brands in his vast news web is Fox News. It is so influential that the President of the United States takes policy advice from its anchors over the recommendations of government officials.

By controlling the news, we can effectively control the narrative of events that people see. Modern news cycles and the internet allow people to suckle off the news feed like a baby on a bottle.

> **Example:** Fox News is well-known for providing a viewpoint dictated by and to conservative Americans. They use this platform to sew fear and hatred by constantly proclaiming that certain groups are "waging war" on American values. They use this fervor to whip up anger against whatever and whoever their target of the day is.

Threats: Violence, restricting freedoms, and other threats can instill fear in a population. These can be lies or threats reflecting actual intentions. However the threats take shape, they can wreak havoc on the mental state of entire populations. The effects of the terror from these threats can last generations beyond the end of the campaign.

> **Example:** The President of the United States and the Supreme Leader of North Korea often threaten each other with nuclear annihilation. This and other threats like it make the entire world quiver in fear.

Leaflets: Paper propaganda is often distributed by hand or dropped from the air. The flyers have manipulative or misleading information on them. These messages are designed to persuade readers to support or oppose political events and legislation.

Example: Memes are a digital form of leaflets that get passed around social media. They have half-truths and outright lies that are so ubiquitous it makes them easy to believe.

Objects: T-shirts, posters, hats, pins, and other physical objects are an effective way to get a message out. They become symbols for larger movements in areas of political, religious, and philosophical interest. The objects often become tools for promotion and worship.

Example: The crucifix is a prime example of a physical object being used as a symbol to encourage worship.

False Flag: A False Flag is when a group releases information or carries out an attack that is fake. These operations instill fear and actively place blame for the event with a different group. These operations often use actors or other knowing participants to further the ruse.

It is almost impossible to prove that something is a false flag operation unless someone involved admits it. There are some indicators, but a skilled operator can avoid them with ease. This makes limiting the number of people involved to the absolute minimum a necessity.

The best part about these operations is that they don't actually need to be real for people to believe them. Simply suggesting that something is a false flag can give people all the push they need to accept the theory.

> **Example:** The U.S. used false flag operations during WW2 to make their enemies believe they wouldn't attack Normandy. When the Allies did land, they found the beaches poorly defended and successfully took them.

Mass Media: It might not seem like it at first but films, books, and music can all be used as tools of psychological warfare. These messages can rewrite history or provide new perspectives/ideas. They can reframe anything from genocide as social advancement to instilling a distrust of a specific government. When done well, this method can provide a highly energized population that is easily and covertly manipulated through other means.

> **Example:** Companies like Facebook and Google openly admit to filtering results and displaying stories they believe will elicit a response. Countries like China, the U.S., and Russia all engage in this technique. Russia was exceptionally successful when it used mass media to influence the 2016 U.S. presidential election.

Chapter 7: Body Language

Humans are adept at reading body language or the nonverbal signals we use to communicate. These nonverbal cues can communicate more information that the words we choose. From facial expressions to how we stand, the things we don't say convey volumes of information.

People have a natural inclination to engage in helping behavior. Our communal nature makes it imperative to understand the meaning behind nonverbal cues. This makes every person on earth a mind reader. It just so happens that some people are better at it than others.

Our communities aren't a big homogenous mass though. We divide up into micro and macro groups and prioritize our "tribe" when making decisions. In the long run, it provides significant benefits to team up rather than every person for themselves.

But our mind-reading abilities add a layer of complexity. Humans can lie or otherwise hide their true intentions. This often provides a significant short-term advantage at the cost of ill will from others in the community.

Deception is an active performance. It requires decent brain power and effort to maintain a ruse for any length of time. We can only focus on a few things at a time so our body language often gives away our true thoughts and intentions.

I have learned a few tricks that can help anyone improve their ability to influence others through body language. They are simple but have helped everyone from vacuum salesmen to Ted Bundy hide their true intentions.

These techniques aren't going to stop racism, misogyny or ass-hats. But they can pressure others to respond in subtle or overt ways. With enough practice and proper execution, they will push people over the fence of suspicion and help you change a no into a yes.

Practice Perfect Posture: When I walk into a room, people immediately know that I am the one in charge. I don't have to tell them I'm in charge, they have already decided I am before I even open my mouth. I communicate this information to them primarily through posture.

Posture communicates our status within a group more than the clothes on our back and the words coming from our mouths. It only takes a second for someone to start making decisions about me. So I make sure to instantly communicate authority and power through the way I hold my body.

I stand and gesture using specific techniques that subtly show dominance and control without seeming like a tyrant or manipulative. These techniques include standing erect, using gestures with palms facing down, and with filling my space.

The brain is programmed to equate power with the amount of

space they take up. Standing straight makes you look taller and holding the shoulders back maximizes the space I take up. But if I slouched, I appear project submission and weakness.

Maintaining good posture helps others understand that I am someone worth knowing. While using my space to make broad and expansive gestures shows others I know my limits. These combine to command respect and help others to value engaging with me.

Adopt a Likable Tone: Coming into an interaction defensively or acting like I want to fight is naturally off-putting. It sets me up to be rejected and makes the other person retract. If my intention is to influence a subject, I need them open and welcoming, not closed and defensive.

So I approach them as an old friend, helping them relax slightly and naturally open up. By showing I am comfortable, it signals to others that they should be as well. It's surprising how welcoming people can be when they relax a bit.

By acting friendly and open, they almost instinctively respond with warmth. They may remain suspicious of your intentions if you overplay it though. So be friendly, not fake, and believe that people want to help.

> **Example:** When I meet someone for the first time, I smile and introduce myself in a familiar way and ask something about them. I begin my encounter on the

basis that we are old friends meeting again. This helps me with the next trick...

Mirror Body Language: One of the most important elements of attraction is believing that the other person understands you on a deep level. The feeling of someone just *getting you* is intoxicating. The more we feel they understand us the deeper our connection.

It's important to emphasize commonalities rather than differences. The more we have in common, the more likely we are to align our motives and goals. These situations show us that the other person is similar to us. Since body language communicates the most information in the shortest time, it's the best way to establish that feeling of similarity.

People naturally mirror body language. We often don't think about our stance, tone, and position in conversation consciously. By monitoring and mirroring the other person's body language, it sets them up to be more attracted to me and value my opinion higher.

> **Example:** Be subtle! If the other person shifts their weight to lean against a wall, lean up against it too. If they talk with their hands, I make sure to gesture when I talk. If they cross their legs, I do the same but in a slightly different position. I don't make huge changes, just enough to be in sync with the other person.

Establish Control: Once we are in sync, I begin to lead the conversation. I continually build rapport and when the time is right I begin changing my body language to encourage them to mirror me. Once they follow my lead, I know that I am in control and can diffuse an intense situation or build excitement.

The fastest way to gain trust is to mirror the other person's body language. Before I start leading, I have to get them to be in sync with me. The better I can do at mirroring and tone, the faster they sync up and I gain control of the conversation.

Questions help establish control of a conversation. It may seem counter-intuitive, but the person giving answers is weaker than the person asking the questions. So I ask questions as often as possible, although I rarely give the other person time to answer them.

Once in control, I can lead the conversation where I want. All the while I watch and study their reactions. I keep tailoring my questions and responses to encourage the other person to respond emotionally. The more emotion I can work up, the more control I have.

> **Example:** If I want to convince a person to sign a contract, I control the conversation by asking questions and mirroring their body language. I'll cross my legs if they cross theirs and make similar gestures as my subject. Once their body language starts syncing up with mine, I ask questions like, "What are you going to do

once you sign?" and "I can't believe we managed to get these terms. You must feel pretty lucky right?"

Make Eye Contact: We are the only primates in the world with white in our eyes. That's because we use them as a primary way to communicate. The eye is called the window to the soul because of how integral it is to body language.

Without good eye contact, people will perceive you as nervous, shifty, or unattractive. Making eye contact with someone creates an intense connection. That connection is integral to appearing trustworthy and engaged.

This doesn't mean to stare people down. Eyes can communicate aggression as easily as timidity. Refusing to break eye contact can make others uncomfortable and appear overly intense.

> **Example:** I maintain eye contact for about 80% of my interactions. When the other person is talking, I maintain eye contact unless they are talking about something in eyesight or are becoming overly excited. I lower my eyes to communicate sadness, raise them for praise and keep my eyes mainly on the speaker.

Give Good Face: When talking about body language, we tend to focus on the torso and limbs. Things like posture, where and when to touch someone and how to hold our hands dominate the conversation. We often underestimate the power of emotive expressions.

It always surprises me how effective a smile is in communicating emotions. It can indicate pleasure, happiness, irony, appeasement, or a superiority complex. A genuine smile is one of the most underrated aspects of attraction.

We are the only primates that smile at people we like. The others see it as a threat display. People naturally find a mouth full of pearly white teeth to be very attractive.

Just make sure any smile you give is genuine. When people realize you are faking a smile, it sours their disposition. It gives away that you are deceiving them and calls everything you do and say into question.

Chapter 8: Deception

In psychology research, deception is a highly debated ethical issue. Some psychologists argue that deceiving people that participate in a research study is dishonest. Yet they cannot deny its effectiveness.

Deception in the real world is very different from what is performed in the lab. In addition to often being long-term in nature, real-world deception actively benefits the liar and may harm the target/victim. This can provide a quantitative difference in the method and veracity of deception between the lab and the real world.

As we talked about in the previous chapter, it is difficult for individuals to completely mask their deception. Body language, cognitive-dissidence, and cultural/sub-cultural norms all "leak" the deceiver's intention to a perceptive target, but there is a multitude of reasons for deception and methods of detection.

Personal morality is a major cause of leakage. In most situations, people rely on both verbal and nonverbal cues to determine the truthfulness of a statement or action. These cues reflect an internal mental state that presumably corresponds to guilt.

There are many types of deception. Some are for personal gain while others are ideological in nature. Other deceptions are performed with the sole purpose of harming a victim. War and sports are venues where deception is considered an asset.

There are five main types of deception. Each performs a different function when trying to persuade. But all require at least a grain of truth in order to pass undetected.

Lies: These are false expressions given with the intent to deceive. They actively misdirect and give false impressions. Lies can be large or small but they are almost always used to escape detection or punishment.

Most cultures have strict moral codes that punish this type of deception. Some codify it into laws with harsh punishments. The United States does this with perjury where lying in court can result in severe repercussions.

> **Example:** If I testify in a trial and the prosecutor asks me, "Did you know the defendant?" and I reply, "No." even though I did, that is a lie. If the lie is discovered, I could face time in prison and a hefty fine.

Equivocations: These are ambiguous statements intended to mislead by representing two different meanings within a single conversation or context. They abuse words and expressions with multiple meanings throughout an argument. The meaning of the word shifts throughout the conversation to mean what the equivocator desires.

Religious clerics and politicians love using this method to

control the faithful. The nature of faith (in a supreme being or the power of people) requires that the definition shift to fit the situation. Languages with many words that have multiple meanings (like English) are easier to do this with than ones without (like Mandarin).

> **Example:** My friend Mike is an atheist and says he has endured persecution for his beliefs. I can then claim that an atheist is by definition one who lacks belief. So Mike can't be persecuted for beliefs he does doesn't hold.

> Here my meaning of the word "belief" changes. It starts by representing the word as the belief in a divine power. Something atheists strictly don't have. But I switch to meaning a deeply held thought or ideal right after. Those are things atheists do have. By using the same word to describe two different meanings, I create ambiguity and misrepresent atheists.

Concealments: These are statements specifically designed to obscure the truth. They hide reality and avoid revealing information the person knows they are expected to disclose. Concealing is normally viewed as less egregious than outright lying but is still frowned upon by most groups and organizations.

This type of deception is most common when someone is getting interrogated. If the other person ever calls me out on concealing something, I can always claim I didn't remember.

Lawyers and salesman are notorious for leaving out key information from their dealings.

> **Example:** Let's assume I am selling a car and I know that the brakes are broken and can't be fixed. Then a prospective buyer asks me "Is there anything wrong with it?" If I tell them, "Everything works as good as the day I got it," I conceal the truth (that the brakes don't work) and open myself up to severe repercussions.

Exaggerations: These are statements that actively inflate reality. They show something is bigger, better, stronger or worse than it really is. There is no limit to how far someone can go, only a threshold of willingness to stretch the truth.

But there are limits to how far the law will let this happen. Advertisers exaggerate in their marketing so much that most governments put limits on what they are allowed to say. Trying to stretch the truth too far has cost more than one evil genius more than they bargained for.

Don't underestimate the effect of exaggeration. It is a powerful way to show differences and make a point. But every time I exaggerate, it becomes less effective so I keep it as a backup or as a debate-ender.

> **Example:** The most common way people exaggerate is to claim that something is impossible. Just because we haven't figured out how to do something doesn't mean it

can't be done. Most of us understand this but still use the exaggerated figure of speech because it is more impactful than saying, "I don't know how to perform this task and have no confidence in my abilities."

Understatements: These statements downplay or minimize the importance of something. This is common in humor and redefines the subject in underwhelming terms. This is helpful to minimize offense and denying intent. Most groups don't mind this as much as other rhetorical devices, and some actually encourage the behavior.

Pretty much anything people compete in condones some level of understatements. Sports, TV shows and other competitions value the ability to keep a strategy secret.

> **Example:** If someone I like bumps into me, I will often use understatements to smooth over the interaction. If they say, "Did I hurt you?" I might respond with "No, I'm fine." Alternatively, saying people killed in a military action are "collateral damage" is an understatement that minimizes the importance of their lives and subsequent deaths.

There is more to deceiving than just lying. Deception is basically defined as a manipulation of appearances such that they give a false sense of reality. It often serves a personal or ideological goal and is carried out over a period of time. Given how broad that definition is, it's hard to find a common set of features that fit all the possible ways to do it.

Deception takes a careful balance of hiding and providing information to keep going. It allows us to carve out a mental path for others to follow and gives us the means to coerce them to follow it. But it must remain undetected by the victims to remain effective.

There are places where deception is sanctioned. Sports competitions, the theater, and interrogations all encourage and endorse the effective use of deception. In these places, there is an implicit contract between the deceiver and the victim.

Doing a good job means fooling onlookers and competitors into having an exaggerated view of you and your talents. Poker tournaments are legendary for how participants try to deceive each other. The only problems with cards come when the players and onlookers don't agree on the acceptable terms.

For these and other reasons, deception generally depends on keeping the intended victim naive to it. But outside of the sanctioned venues, society reacts poorly to deception.

Jokes, fantasies, teasing and sharing social lies are little deceptions that find a degree of tolerance. This implies that the severity of the reaction has a close relation to the perceived harm they do to others in that society.

Military and strategic deception are regularly sponsored by the state. There isn't a nation in history that didn't engage in some form of this behavior. They understand that the best way to preserve their way of life is to win.

The need to train in war and deception actually led to many of the sports we know today. Fencing, football, tennis, and polo all developed because people needed a sanctioned way to train in the arts of war. Sports are essentially battles where the combatants agree not to kill each other and then making up rules from there.

Many of the tactics developed on the battlefield transfer to civilian and love life. There are con artists, cheaters, liars, and thieves everywhere. Being familiar with their tactics allows me to defend myself from their deceptions.

Once we recognize the situation for what it is, we have a chance to win the day, and that takes a combination of preparation and execution to accomplish. Winning the day can be anything from defeating an enemy to scoring an ally, or having sex.

People are unique and what works well for one person might not be as effective with another. It can take some flexibility to keep a target engaged and committed, so here are a few final ways to win the day.

Gather Information: As discussed in previous chapters, body language and cognition play key roles in interpersonal communication. Watching, listening, and mirroring the subject all provide valuable insight into how to persuade them. Gathering as much useful information as possible gives you the biggest advantage.

Just don't get too bogged down in the details. They matter but only if you get enough of them. Remember that it's better to have many data points that approximate reality than a single data point that fits reality.

Example:

Strategic Show of Vulnerability: It's incredible how powerful a well-timed show of weakness is. Such displays can deflect suspicion or encourage feelings of trust and attraction.

Calling attention to a weakness shows potential allies that I understand I'm not perfect. It also gives others the feeling that they have some control over me. But I don't reveal just any old weakness.

The revealed weakness needs to be something that is both visible and easily reinforced. This gives the impression of invulnerability when you are able to overcome it (if only slightly). That perceived strength can be the difference between getting what you want and not.

> **Example:** I use the information I gathered to choose a weakness that I have taken steps to cover or is otherwise negated. That way I can distract others from the weaknesses I can't see and don't know how to negate. In

the end, it's normally better to see your opponent or lover coming than not.

Don't Reveal the Plan: It isn't deception if you tell everyone all about it. Keeping things quiet ensures nobody takes steps to stop your plans. They also can't report what they don't know.

Sometimes other people are a necessity. Try to tell other people as little as possible—basically just enough to allow them to accomplish their part of the plan. Limiting the number of people who know about the evil you plan to unleash is a key part of keeping it from leaking to the wrong people.

Disney villains always lose in part because they reveal their evil plan. Likewise, real people end up behind bars because they talk about the crazy shit they've done. Once you put that out there, you can't take it back.

Police often use sworn testimony against defendants in court. Self-incrimination is such a common problem that the U.S. put protections against it in the Bill of Rights. It's not as "gotcha" in real life as on TV but it is still one of the biggest blunders a person can make.

> **Example:** Nobody remembers Ted Bundy for his political contributions. They remember him for cutting up a bunch of people and getting caught. He couldn't help but give himself away as a truly evil person and once he did, his life behind bars began.

Conclusion

Psychology opens the gates to human understanding. Because of our long and violent history as a species, we all have dark parts lying within ourselves. This book shows you how people tap into that hidden strength and put it to use.

Most can agree that an evil person is one whose objective gains get significantly outweighed by the injury and damage that person caused—someone with full responsibility for the actions and clearly intended to violate moral norms.

The techniques described in this book outline the methods that people use to influence, manipulate, and otherwise control every one of us. They are cold, callous, and often ignore the moral implications of using them. It highlights the reason and method behind those evil acts without judgment or encouragement.

Using these methods improperly will land you in prison, if not worse. But understanding the limits and depths of human control will help you recognize when others are attempting to control you.

This book walks you through the most powerful dark psychology techniques there are. It teaches everything you need to know about persuasion, NLP, CBT, social manipulation, subliminal messaging, psychological warfare, body language, and deception.

There are no frills, no filler, and no BS. I lay it out and give solid examples of how these techniques are used. I highlight their strengths and talk about their limitations and how to overcome them. Every chapter is packed with real-world methods for dominating any situation.

Manipulation

-Dark Psychology-

How to Analyze People and Influence Them to Do Anything You Want Using NLP and Subliminal Persuasion

inattention, use or misuse of the information in question by the reader will render any resulting actions solely under their purview. There are no scenarios in which the publisher or the original author of this work can be in any fashion deemed liable for any hardship or damages that may befall them after undertaking information described herein.

Additionally, the information in the following pages is intended only for informational purposes and should thus be thought of as universal. As befitting its nature, it is presented without assurance regarding its prolonged validity or interim quality. Trademarks that are mentioned are done without written consent and can in no way be considered an endorsement from the trademark holder.

Introduction

Congratulations on purchasing *Manipulation: Dark Psychology-How to Analyze People and Influence Them to Do Anything You Want Using NLP and Subliminal Persuasion* and thank you for doing so.

The chapters that follow will provide you with all you'll need to know to bend people's ideas to your will. You'll learn three different techniques of dark psychology that will become the primary tools you'll need. You'll first learn about neuro-linguistic programming, or NLP. This will build the foundation for everything else, so it's important to understand it first. Even if you skip over the other chapters, make sure you remember not to skip chapter one. The second is subliminal persuasion, which is something you are quite familiar with, even if you don't know it. Every time you buy a candy bar because the package looks nice, you fall for this persuasion. The third is a discussion on cold reading. This is another tactic you have at least heard before. Every time you hear about a medium, a psychic, or watch a detective movie, you hear about cold reading. Here you'll not only learn what it is, but how you can use it to your own advantage. Beyond that you'll learn about different ways you can analyze people both from afar and up close so that you may learn the best ways to work with them before the final chapter puts it all together. Within the final chapter are different tips, tricks, and techniques to achieve what you want.

There are plenty of books on this subject on the market, thanks again for choosing this one. Every effort was made to ensure it is full of as much useful information as possible, please enjoy.

Chapter 1: Neuro-Linguistic Programming: What is NLP?

Background:

Created by Richard Bandler and John Grinder in the 1970's, neuro-linguistic programming, or NLP, has been discussed by scientists, hypnotists, and even users of parlor trick "magic". NLP has been used in alternative medicine to treat illnesses like Parkinson's disease. It has also been used in psychotherapy, advertisement, sales, management, coaching, teaching, team building, and public speaking. Yes, each one of these categories is a form of manipulation to some degree. You can't go to a class, the grocery store, or even a restaurant without being subject to some form of manipulation. No matter where you are you can't escape it. It's present in advertisement posters, the tactic of that business sales clerk that stops you at the mall, the product placement in the movie you're watching, and everywhere else. However, instead of being afraid of this knowledge, you can use it to your advantage and redirect that manipulation as the wielder.

However, you didn't buy this book to learn what other people can use NLP for. You want to know the benefits to yourself, correct? Well to properly put NLP to use and manipulate people to do your bidding, you need to understand how NLP works and what steps you need to take to reach the final stage of persuasion. This chapter explains exactly what you need to know step-by-step, beginning with rapport building.

Building Rapport with Someone

Just as a therapist begins their treatment plan by building rapport with their clients, you need to build a foundation of trust with the person you wish to persuade. You won't take a lot of advice from that therapist if they begin firing off life changes and new rules to follow the moment you sit down at your first session. You'll likely leave seconds later, and that therapist's career won't last much longer. The same rules apply when you want to work manipulation on another person. It's important to be attentive and listen to what the other person is saying. Watch their body language and listen to their words. You'll need this information for the chapter on analysis, as what a person says and how they act is vital to understanding them. Develop some trust by behaving in an honest, and genuine way. Be warm and friendly so you're comfortable to be around. Every person is a little different, and each mind is made up of a series of events, situations, and experiences that make up who they are. Without some of this crucial information, you won't know exactly which strategies to use when the time comes to persuade them. To gain this information, you need to develop a relationship with them.

Listen and Watch

This is the most time-consuming step, as it is the basis of building the structure for the more intimate relationship you'll build later. You can do this with the use of psychoanalysis, which is explained more in-depth in chapter four. You will need to learn this person's body language, emotions, history, and reactions to stress. Body language is essential to NLP practices. Not only is it vital to the beginning, but, knowing how to read body language comes into play all throughout the NLP process and any other psychological process. Luckily, the longer you build a relationship with someone, the easier it will be to know their tells, as they are developed from habit. Some people may be guarded around you, which will appear as tense or straight shoulders and back, not holding your gaze, or even fidgeting. This is a sign you aren't building the vital rapport. Before moving any further, this person needs to feel relaxed and warm around you. Watch for an open face, a relaxed smile, and some easy-going interaction such as light laughter. Stay away from heavy topics until this person is comfortable with you.

Watching for a person's emotions can be tricky, as people don't feel only one at a time. Their surface emotion, which is what you can easily read, is displayed on their face and in their body language. For instance, if a person is feeling irritated, their face will be tight, their eyes will be downcast, and they may cross their arms over their chest. What is below the surface, is often more complicated. Depending on how well this person has developed their ability to hide emotion, it may be guarded closely and well hidden. Emotions that are deeper can be loneliness, grief, or anxiousness. Getting to know these deeper emotions will take time, observation, and trust.

When it comes to emotions, the best place to watch is a person's eyes. Many have called eyes the gate-way to the soul and have done so with good reason. Emotion is often displayed in the eyes in some form. If a person is happy, their eyes are held more open and the extra light creates the sparkling illusion that is often referenced with happiness in eyes. If a person feels defeated or exhausted, their lids hover lower over their eyes, which will cause them to appear darker. The eyes will also show you how close your connection really is, as eye contact is a major indicator that people are genuine and listening to your words.

Enthusiasm is a key factor with persuasion. While getting to know someone, let some passion out. Those who are passionate about certain subjects appear as natural leaders. When trying to persuade someone, you'll need to use a certain level of enthusiasm, however it shouldn't appear misplaced in the moment. When someone is speaking, show interest. This trait should appear when the other person is discussing their personal interests, as well as when you display your own.

Express your passions. When you want to convince them on something later, you'll need some of that intense passion to successfully sell them on your idea.

Stress responses, which are important to understand, appear in three different ways. Overcompensating, such as acting strong and unaffected during a time of grief, under compensating, which is the act of giving obvious tells of an emotion, and coping mechanisms. Overcompensating, and under compensating are universally similar and are usually east to spot. If you see someone acting abnormally happy in a less-than-happy situation, it's safe to say they are overcompensating. If a gloomy person is almost theatrical with displaying their sour mood, they are undercompensating. Both come out for varying reasons, and not everyone is aware they are doing it. Coping mechanisms, however, develop over time and usually occur from an act, or series of acts, of trauma. A common coping mechanism is pushing those away who may want to get emotionally close. This mechanism usually develops from the repeated act of betrayal, teaching a young individual that anyone who wishes to be loving to them has a darker ulterior motive and they cannot be trusted. Breaking through these barriers will lead to a deeper relationship and a closer connection. You'll also see a more open version of the other person, and their words will be more genuine. The way to do this is to be honest when this person least expects it and remain present. If the coping mechanism doesn't work, the person will eventually stop trying.

Act with Honesty

Giving the illusion of honesty and acting with genuine intent behind each action will cause you to appear real and trustworthy. Remember, surprise them by being honest when it is least expected. That way, you'll seem a genuine person by nature. By now, you should know this person's body language well enough to copy it as your own. Don't do so obviously, however, as it may appear mocking. Mirroring some of the other's body language will make this person more open to what you are saying without them consciously knowing it. You'll seem relatable as well, which will strengthen the connection you've been building. Another way to become relatable is by sharing some personal information. When someone senses vulnerability in another, they will feel more inclined to become vulnerable in response. By now this relationship should be deeper and more intimate. you can begin using techniques of manipulation.

The word "manipulation" is often viewed as a negative word and filed strictly under the category of immoral. The sad truth is that manipulation often is used for morally wrong reasons and in cruel ways. However, the way manipulation is used depends entirely upon how you use it. You could use manipulation to help a person just as much as you can to harm them. For instance, I knew a person who had grown up with a broken relationship with her father. A year before he died, she learned that his time living was limited, however she made no indication that she was going to see or speak with him. Having already developed a close relationship with her, I knew her emotions were scattered on the subject, and her word choices such as "would have" and "might have" suggested a part of her wanted to speak with him and gain some closure about his parental choices. She was adamant about leaving things as they were and letting him pass without a word spoken between them. I offered her a similar story I had been through and emphasized how much healthier I felt as a person when I let all of my feelings out. I even reasoned that he might have an apology or explanation that might help her to understand him if she speaks with him. I emphasized that nothing he can say excuses his action, though understanding why they happened might help her move on. She did have a conversation with him and has thanked me on multiple occasions, as she learned of his crippling mental illness. Overselling a point, as I did, approaching the person in a relatable manner, and offering logical information are tactics that can persuade another to see your point as logical. Had I not explained my own personal story, she may have chosen not to speak with her father despite my logical points. I had used my persuasive skills to help her improve her own views on her father and offer some comfort before he passed on. Though my actions are viewed as manipulation, how I used it wasn't immoral.

There are gray areas when it comes to manipulation of course, as often the reason to persuade someone is because they don't want to do as you suggest. Sometimes, the only person who can make the judgement call on whether or not the act is morally sound, is you. Use these skills with your best judgement and plan out any consequences before you act so you don't end up with regrets.

Chapter 2: Subliminal Persuasion

In our world, subliminal persuasion is everywhere. You can't watch television, read a magazine, or even go for a drive around town without encountering it. The definition of subliminal persuasion is the use of objects, photos, words, or another means of persuading someone into doing something or putting an idea in their head without them consciously knowing what you've done. A common example of this is advertising. When you see or hear the points made when someone is trying to sell you a product, your mind may think of the product as appealing. You usually won't know that the techniques used in the advertisement itself are the reason you feel like you need their product. Often you wouldn't have bought this item otherwise. Below is an example of how this advertising technique works.

Picture this:

A glass of soda is displayed in front of you surrounded by warm colors. It is perfectly carbonated, as there is an emphasis on the infinite bubbles working their way to the top of the bottle. As it is being opened, the sound of carbon being released rushes from the bottle. It is a perfect day without a cloud in sight, and golden rays of sun are shining overhead. The glare of the sun is shining on the pristine glasswork. The drink is so cold in contrast with the warm day that precipitation has formed into fat drops of water that are slowly sliding down the glass and following the way it's perfectly shaped to fit a hand. As a model brings the drink to their lips, just a drop escapes and slides down her chin and it catches the golden light of the sun as it falls, slowly out of the frame. The model's eyes slide closed slowly with pure bliss and satisfaction. The camera zeros in on the muscles of her neck contracting and stretching; and as she puts the drink down a smile forms on her face.

You might not be in a warm area, nor may you particularly want a soda right now. However, that description was followed by your mind and you may feel thirstier than before you read it. This is because my words used subliminal persuasion to make you want the soda that was described. You've seen advertisements like this many of times, and they might have worked. Never does a cold drink display so much precipitation as it does on the picture of an advertisement unless it has been sitting in water. However, because the body craves liquid when we are even a little dehydrated, the look will appeal to that natural desire. Even if what your body wants is water, this advertisement will appeal because of the unrealistic water droplets that have formed on the can or bottle.

When using this tactic in the form of manipulating another person, there are a few different ways to go about it. For instance, if you create a sense of "we" and equality in the request, it feels more inclusive. When sales clerks and advertisers work, they often create the idea that the product benefits both them and you as a consumer. They speak as if by buying their product, you not only get the benefit of having the product they think you need, but they will be happier for it. If you word the request in a form that appeals to both you and the other person, you're more likely to achieve your goal. This form of persuasion can also combine well with cold reading techniques, as both involve the other person believing something without you outright offering the information to them. Cold reading is explained further in the next chapter, as well as an example of how it can be used to put an idea in someone's mind to demonstrate how it can benefit anyone in the sales industry.

Another form of persuasion is gathering favors. Debt is a constant in this world, and it doesn't always mean money. If you've done something for the other person recently, and have earned a form of gratitude, they're likely to feel indebted to you and therefore, more obligated to carry out your request. For example, if you save this person from an embarrassing situation, such as lending them a jacket when they've spilt a drink down their shirt, you may request a favor in return later on. Because you displayed a kindness for no apparent reason that they can see, they'll feel the need to retaliate the kindness. Favors can be as large as saving someone's life, or even as small as some good advice. Every act doesn't need to be an all-out sacrifice. In fact, it shouldn't be. If someone catches a hint of deception or ulterior motives when someone is displaying such kindness, they will feel distrustful towards you, and you will lose your relationship that you've worked towards by now. Every act, as mentioned in chapter one, must feel and appear genuine.

You can use this kind of persuasion technique yourself to get people to do as you wish, provided you do so subtly. Examples and tips on how to do this will be discussed in more depth in chapter five.

Chapter 3: Cold Reading

Cold reading is known to be a con artist's best friend. It provides the illusion of mind reading and magical abilities without the use of actual supernatural power. It is often used by those who make a living through fortune-telling and psychic acts. Many people have been completely sold on the act, as it is usually performed by someone who excels in reading others, has acquired enough general knowledge, and has practiced enough to deliver a very believable performance. However, such an act is really only a form of psychology, and you could create this act yourself if you chose to. You would do this by creating the illusion of knowing more than you really do through the power of observation. There are different names for the different techniques. How many people are present decides how you should approach it. Shot gunning, for instance, is done in a large room packed with people. This is often the choice of mediums who are creating the illusion of connecting to a passed loved one, because whatever they say, there is likely to be someone who can relate to the statement. When the medium speaks a few, usually vague, phrases, such as "I am connecting to an elderly man... the name John or Jack comes to mind. Does that speak to anyone?" he or she watches for anyone who expresses recognition. The names Jack and John are very common, and many people have lost a grandfather in

MANIPULATION AND DARK PSYCHOLOGY

their time. The medium will then choose one person and watch their face carefully. This is where the true psychology steps in. Reading body language is essential to keeping up the ruse, as the medium will need to narrow down the descriptions of the audience members loved one. If, for example, the medium says something about a white picket fence, yet no familiarity comes to this person's face, he or she will have to carefully change their tactic. He or she might explain that he never lived within a white picket fence, but wanted to, or that another relative was also present. If the audience member agrees or seems excited, this medium will know they are getting warmer. This act is continued, and even peppered by what are known as rainbow ruses. These are contradictory phrases such as "He was a gentle man, however he would occasionally display a stern side". Most people have experienced these contradictory moments in their personality, however the word choice feels so specific that it seems as if it only applies to the supposed spirit the man or woman is referring to.

Another method of cold reading, which may be more suitable to a smaller population, is to use previous knowledge when observing someone's behavior. This method is often used in detective dramas, as the act is dramatic and exciting to watch, and the character appears intelligent and clever. It is, however, easier than it may appear, as it only takes keen observation skills. For example, if you meet a new person and notice there is graphite smudged along the side of their left hand, you will know that they are left-handed, as those who are left-hand dominant must drag their hand along the previously written words to continue writing. As a left-hander myself, I would know. This phenomenon, which has been jokingly called "The Silver Surfer Syndrome", is an unquestionable indication that this person is left-handed, and you may say so with confidence as you shake their hand. The confident statement will shock this person, and they won't think to look for physical indicators. This can be used as a fun trick to amuse others, or as a shocking factor to carry into a persuasive technique, as those who have recently been surprised don't always think every factor of a decision through.

Cold reading, as any other manipulation tactic, can be used on anyone. And it is. Many people who are studied in the ways of cold reading have used it as a career, such as psychics, fortune-tellers, and any kind of con artist. Such a complicated set-up is not necessary to add this skill to your own toolbox, as you only need your own observation and shock factor. Another example is if you see someone you may already know is a student, you could confidently exclaim that they were studying late and fell asleep on their work as you note the imprint of math work on their left ear. These subtle observations build up over time, and you may gain a reputation with that person. The more you get to know someone, the more background information you will have stored away. For example, say you have a friend named Kyle. Kyle is a single father of an adorable six-year old girl whom he spends every moment he can with. To support her, he works at a grueling desk job where he files paperwork all day long and takes rude phone calls. You know that he likes light coffee with a lot of sweetener, and that he is right-handed.

Today, Kyle arrives with a large coffee in his left hand. You two always meet up every Tuesday around ten in the morning. Today, it's almost eleven. In the back of his car is a pink hairbrush. When he gets close enough to greet you, you smell the strong aroma of black coffee rising from his cup, and you can see his clothes are wrinkled. Without asking him, what can you deduce from his situation?

I believe that his boss kept him very late and piled on the work the night prior. He's gotten papercuts before, however even the light touch of his coffee seems to be too much pain this time, so he was working as quickly as he could. Even so, he got home late that night and overslept the next morning. Rushing to get her to school, Kyle likely tossed his daughter's hairbrush back for her to do her best with her hair on their way to school. Due to his exhaustion, he stopped to buy a coffee much stronger than he likes it before meeting with you. Of course, there are other indicators that weren't mentioned in the example. What situations you come to find yourselves observing will vary, as will the indicators that you notice.

You can also use cold reading to gather information you don't really have, by acting as if you do. For example, if you are a

99

business salesman in a clothing shop who encounters a shy, young girl that is close to the age of high school, you may focus on this observation to begin with. You could state or ask with confidence if she has an event coming up. It doesn't hurt to be aware of large school events nearby either, as there may be a dance she wants to prepare for. She may nod or shrug. Either response isn't a no. After, you could press on and ask if she wants to wear something that will catch a certain someone's attention. Because she's shy, she may have difficulty speaking about her feelings to that cute boy from her math class. Or, she may even want to look nice to feel superior to that girl who bullies her about her looks. Either way, this vague statement will technically be correct. With this much information, you can gather that she'll want to look elegant. Taking a look at her clothes that she currently has on will give you a clue as to her preference with style. If she's wearing long sleeves, and baggy pants, she won't feel inclined to wear something revealing. You can work with this in two ways. You could persuade her to buy the dress with a low back and no sleeves by explaining how confident she'll appear while that yellow brings out the color in her eyes, or you could take the safer approach and find her a nice dress with long sleeves and a high neckline. This whole time, the girl never told you what she actually wanted or why she needed a dress, but you learned enough to make the sale anyway.

Cold reading isn't only useful in sales clerk settings and parlor tricks. You can also use it to gain a favor, shock someone into doing as you wish, and learning enough about another person to use to your advantage. In chapter five, more examples on how you can use cold reading to sway people your way will be delved into.

Chapter 4: Analysis

In any kind of persuasion tactic, analyzing people is the key to hit or miss when it comes to success or failure. You can analyze a person by their word choice, their behavior, their vibes, their body language, and even their appearance. Each will be explained in detail in this chapter, as well as examples and stories on how you can apply this knowledge yourself. Remember, even if a persuasion trick doesn't explicitly state to observe the person, you still should, as the best information you could obtain is through analysis. You can learn about a person's mood, some of their history, some personality traits, and even their attitude towards different situations simply by observing them. It's important to understand analysis, so absorb this information and take it with you to the final chapter, where you'll learn how to use all of these techniques for persuasion.

Word Choice

The words people chose to use in any given situation can tell a lot about them, such as their thoughts, feelings, and attitudes. The structure of which a person frames their written or spoken sentences are key indicators of what they thought or felt of the spoken event, and even who they are as a person. If you pay attention to the chosen words that weren't necessary to form a correct sentence, you'll notice that there are a variety of options that person could have chosen. The fact that they deliberately opted for a certain word speaks volumes about who they are and what they think. For example, the sentence, "I worked on the paper," can be changed in a variety of ways. All will still say, plainly that someone worked on a paper, however, each variation will tell you what they thought of the act, and how well they performed it. If that person were to say, "I worked hard on the paper," the word 'hard' indicates that they take pride in the work they put in. This person strives for success and sets goals for themselves to achieve. This paper was viewed by this person as a challenge that they took on and put great effort into overcoming. On the other hand, if someone states, instead, "I worked on the stupid paper," they are showing great resentment. Perhaps this is a student in a class they dislike, and they barely felt inclined to acknowledge the paper, let alone put any effort into it. This person is likely the type who would rather spend their time on something he or she enjoys and finds little value in work that doesn't immediately benefit them. Unlike the hard worker mentioned before, this person is more lax in their work ethic and succeeds in other areas of life than academics.

Different statements create different meanings. Simple statements such as, "I earned an award" suggests that this person believes success is earned and not given, versus the common statement, "I won an award". You can learn a lot about a person by listening to what they choose to say. For example, when I was still in my high school years, I observed a young girl barely younger than I was at the time. She was discussing a teacher with a small group of students. The trio were very loud with their declarations, which indicated that they didn't mind the possibility of others hearing them, nor did they worry such opinions may come back around on them. The girl stood with a defiance in her body language, something that will be discussed later on, and she held her head high. She said, "Mr. Borrock is a moron. I don't know who gave him a teaching degree, but he doesn't know what he's talking about!" To which the girl standing directly across from her snickered and replied, "I know. I transferred to Ms. Ally's class because she's a lot better. She doesn't even grade the homework! If you turn it in, you get an A. Much better than Borrock."

Of course, I changed the names for security reasons, but the statements themselves are what is important. Using only the statement from the first girl, you can imagine that she values her own opinion over anyone else's. She deliberately uses demeaning language when describing her teacher, and even denounces his teaching credibility. By stating that Mr. Borrock "Doesn't know what he's talking about," she is insinuating that she learns nothing from his teachings. This statement points to an arrogance, and a lack of respect to authority. The second girl eagerly agrees with the first, however her take on the situation is greatly different. She boasts that Ms. Ally is a better teacher, however this statement isn't backed up by her teaching method and how much she is learning in her class. She prefers this teacher that is more casual in her grading strategy. These words indicate that she takes minimal pride in her education and finds little to no value in learning. Because this conversation stems from the group of students feeding off of each other's comments, they all are gregarious in nature and feel more comfortable and confident to reveal their opinions in a group.

There are many other ways to read word choices and phrases people choose to use. Always watch for the difference between phrases like, "I like him, and, "I'm fond of him," as 'like' is a very general word that can vary in meaning. Often it is used as a placement word for a lack of real emotion. If you like something, you may range from tolerating it to enjoying it. Without a real indication, however, it usually indicates the former. Fondness, however, is a true emotion. If you are fond of someone, you enjoy being around them. Other differences are, "I bought you a gift," and "I bought you another gift," as the word 'another' indicates resentment or strongly hints at the need for gratitude. This is a strong display of a person in need of power. By learning people's words, you will be learning them.

Body Language

Many professions require the need to learn general body language. Agents in the criminal justice field must know the difference between the behavior of someone innocent, and that of a criminal. Psychiatrists must know how their sessions are making their client feel, so they must know the difference between a person with their head down and their eyes hidden, and someone who is making eye contact openly. Whatever the reason, the study of body language isn't uncommon. Even so, it is important when you are trying to persuade someone. If a person is rigid and looking down, it isn't a good moment to ask something of them, as they are guarded, and their mind is elsewhere. If they are looking at you with relaxed shoulders and their body is facing you, however, they trust you and are genuinely interested in what you are saying. This is a preferable moment to ask a favor than the previous example. If someone is sitting across from you, you can tell their opinion of you based solely on how they are sitting. For example, if their arms are crossed, they are feeling uncomfortable. If they lean away from you, they don't care much for your presence. Whether or not someone consistently looks at you is always a huge indicator, as eye contact is important for a conversation in many countries. If this person is covering their hands somehow, be it stuffing them in their pockets, holding them in their lap under the table, or folding them behind their backs, it usually means they are hiding something. If a person is picking at their cuticles or nails, biting their lips or nails, or fidgeting in their seat, they are displaying discomfort. This can be created from a lie, nervousness in an awkward situation, or a difficult topic of conversation.

For example, if you are having a casual conversation with someone, and they are leaning towards you slightly, and looking at your face, they are interested and engaged in the conversation. However, if you ask a personal matter that this person would rather not speak about, he or she may scratch the back of their neck, bite their lip, or run his or her thumb along their other hand. They might also look down, and their shoulders will hunch forward in a manner that is considered curling into themselves. These signs indicate that the subject is uncomfortable, and possibly off limits at that time. Unless they state they would like to continue, it is best to steer the subject to a safer place until the relationship builds more. If someone feels their privacy is invaded, they will block you out and you will need to redevelop the rapport you had built.

Behavior

A person, or animal's behavior tells you a lot about them. In the wild, experts watch certain behaviors for study to understand the wild animal and the way they live more accurately. A wildlife specialist may watch as young cheetah cubs wrestle each other and will explain that they are playing in a form that is productive to survival, as they are training to fight and hunt. An adult lion will often pretend to be harmed as their child playfully attacks them to promote hunter instinct and ability. A runt of a litter may be excluded from the family in certain activities, as it is a liability and the weakest link.

These same observations may be turned towards humans as well. An example is the common feuding of siblings. As the older sibling, I personally feel that, as a general rule, younger siblings can be spotted a mile away. They tend to make their complaints heard more loudly than those who are older siblings, and they grow up to be much more competitive. A person who was born as the youngest sibling may also be laxer in their ethics and drive to be productive, as parents usually aren't as strict in their discipline by the time the younger children are born. However, I have met many people who swear that they know what an older sibling looks like. I've been told we older siblings act like the parent to everyone around us, as we were the born babysitters of the family. I've also been told that, with the resentment toward the lax parenting of the younger siblings, we tend to need control. I personally don't see it, which is an obvious sign that it must apply to me as well.

Other than birth order, you can also learn desires from behaviors. I once walked around the mall with a couple of friends of mine. Both were female. Upon passing a store filled with cartoon and videogame characters, all three of us ran through the door and nearly squealed at every object with a character we like displayed on it. My shortest friend insisted on buying friendship charms that produce obvious excitement from all of us. A month later, I walked past that same store with a male friend whose interests couldn't differ more than my female companions. Not wanting to appear childish, I purposely did not look at that store or make a comment about it. Had he been paying attention, my friend would have noticed my straighter shoulders and back, my folded hands, and my sudden lack of interest in my surroundings. Being a curious person by nature, I often look around me. My desire that could have been noticed, at that time, was to hide something about myself from my friend.

Behaviors can be subtle as well. Coping mechanisms are behaviors which, as mentioned in chapter one, appear from a trauma. If a person is naturally cold toward older men and acts even more so as they become more integrated into that person's life, they could have had a broken relationship with their father, a close uncle, or a father-figure in their life. The friend I mentioned in chapter one that I persuaded to see her dying father behaved that way around older men. When around a friendly man her eyes would narrow, her shoulders would hunch, and she kept as much distance as she could without appearing outright rude.

Because behaviors develop over time, they tend to indicate deeper information about a person than the other analysis techniques. You'll know what really makes this person tick if you observe enough of them.

Vibes

There's always going to be debate on whether or not "vibes" exist and what they really are. Many deny them as a made-up concept of those same magic users who manipulate people with their cold reading. Others brush it off as nonsense that people choose to believe in. The universal truth, however, is that people give off a feeling when you are around them. Whatever you want to call it, it is there. Some people give off vibes that make you feel happier and generally better than before you were around them. Those people tend to have many others flock around them because the feeling is infectious. These people are often gregarious and smile often. Other people, on the other hand, are known in more spiritual communities as "Energy Vampires". These people's presences tend to "suck" the feeling away from others. These people tend to carry a dark mood with them, and often hold their heads down and even speak with negative intent. An Energy Vampire may frequently make side remarks such as "She's such a suck-up" in regard to a friendlier person asking another if they require assistance. It's important to learn what your vibes are so you know how approachable you are and whether or not you exude that feeling of positivity that draws people in.

Appearance

Strangely enough, appearance can tell you a lot about someone. Though the phrase "don't judge a book by its cover" has circulated through everyone's mind since childhood, you really can learn a lot about that book simply by looking over the cover. If you see a man sitting at a coffee shop wearing a neatly pressed suit with his hair combed neatly atop his head, you can safely assume that he is a man who cares about the opinions of those around him. Unless he's waiting patiently for another man for a meeting, he has no obligation to dress as he does. People who take this much care in their appearance usually also stand with a high posture and put value and pride in their work. They may also thrive on high praise when it comes to their careers and follow social rules such as arriving early, practicing diligence, and always remaining patient. This is a main reason it is a known rule to dress professional to any kind of job interview, regardless of the dress code once you're hired.

On the other hand, a person who dresses more casually puts comfort above outside appearance. This person may care only for personal comforts or pleasures when all other duties have been taken care of or no immediate responsibilities are taking his or her time. Though this person may put effort into their work, they may tend to take their time and won't frequently prioritize work above all else. This person may often be late to events or become distracted often.

Of course, it is unwise to make inferences on anyone on appearance alone. It is simply a tool you can combine with the other methods described in this chapter. For example, say a woman is at a grocery store wearing a simple, stained shirt, and sweatpants and her hair is thrown out of the way without a care as to what it looks like. She is pushing a cart full of baby diapers, children's toys, ingredients to make a meal, and exhaustion is written all over her face. By clothing alone, she might appear lazy and uncaring. However, if you consider the child products of different ages as well as groceries, it is safe to assume she is pressed for time and resources. Appearance just isn't high on her priorities.

On the other hand, if this same woman was standing at an aisle without any urgency, buying little, visibly nervous, and giving off the vibes associated with an Energy Vampire, that might be a different story.

You may choose to judge a book by its cover, however it is important to test a couple of pages as well as the description to make certain before deciding whether or not to buy it.

Chapter 5: Persuasion

By now, you've learned about the basics of NLP, subliminal persuasion, cold reading, and different aspects of analysis that you can use to understand and get to know people without interacting with them directly. Now, the question is, how can you really use these skills to manipulate them into doing your bidding? Well, there are many different ways that incorporate all of these skills without ethical or moral risk to yourself. This chapter explains different tricks to really persuade another that will incorporate everything you have learned from this book. There are different ways you can approach a situation, and each one calls for a different tactic or approach. It's important to know multiple ways of persuading others, and examples of these situations are provided in this chapter. However, it is important to remember these rules that apply to every persuasive trick.

Be Observant

You can't get anywhere if you don't pay attention to your surroundings, the situation, or, most importantly, the person you are trying to persuade. Mood, behavior, and the situation must be appropriate for the moment for the trick to be affective. Remember how to read body language and know how to read this person before you attempt to manipulate them into anything. For example, in one tactic that will be described in this chapter, the key to success is to keep the person focused on the conversation. If you aren't paying attention for the passion and attention needed to make the trick work, you will be caught and your success is unlikely. Attention and observation is key to manipulation.

Honesty and Trustworthiness

No one is going to follow the advice or suggestion of someone they don't trust. Even if the situation doesn't call for rapport or a pre-developed relationship, you need to appear trustworthy. Remember the indicators of discomfort and lying when it comes to body language and avoid them when speaking. If you're telling a half truth or even lying to get what you want from someone, you can't do so while holding your hands behind your back and shifting your weight from one foot to the other. If you can, be genuinely honest, especially if the other person won't expect it. If you seem trustworthy and reliable, people will respond accordingly.

Now that you know all you need to for success, listed below are different examples of how you can persuade someone to do what you want. These techniques range from small favors to large ideas, and each has been drawn from a different source. You'll have a tactic for each occasion, and if you follow the rules listed above and remember all of the knowledge you've gained in this book, you will be successful and gain every advantage you need to get what you desire.

Oversell Your Idea

An NLP tactic used often in the sales industry is to use intense passion to hype-up the idea you want to sell someone on. It's a common practice seen by anyone trying to sell a product, and it works. I've been roped into buying something I regretted many times based entirely on the sales technique. I'm still upset that that skin cream didn't give me perfect skin. When you exaggerate the benefits of an idea and put emphasis on the main points that could sell it, your logic seems sound and it's hard to argue. If someone doesn't really need something, don't tell them *that* they need it, explain *why* they need it. Don't even go near the idea of giving them the option. If you want someone to donate to your favorite organization, tell them how doing so will benefit them just as much as it will help benefitting the organization itself. Set them up for following through before they even know what it is you want to propose. This technique works well when you want someone to take something, which is why it is taught to all sales clerks and is used in advertisements. It also works well with the opposite technique, which is oversimplifying the idea.

Oversimplify Your Idea

If the idea is complicated and contains drawbacks, it might

benefit you to oversimplify it. Oversimplification, by definition, is to leave out information and simplify what you do include until it is distorted. To do this in persuasion, you adjust what you should explain when it comes to your idea. If you want someone to take martial arts lessons with you, but you know that they don't care much for bumps and bruises, you could try this technique. Describe the benefits of learning a martial art. You could explain how you'll both be more active and fit, you'll have the means to defend yourself in an emergency, and you'll learn moves to show off should the occasion arise. Maybe offer to show a few videos of successful martial arts techniques that are visually appealing. If you use enough passion when selling your points, the idea of minor injury might not even occur to your friend. Though, in the case of this example, they might not thank you for it later.

Put Yourself in a Neutral Position

If possible, maintain the illusion of neutrality and limit any perceived bias. For example, if your friend's girlfriend had been begging him to cut his hair for a while, so he looks to you for a second opinion, you shouldn't express any real interest. If you have a quarrel with his hair length, you might say that either way it doesn't matter to you, however, the length indicated in his girlfriend's picture would frame his face well, and in the coming hot weather it will prevent possible heat stroke. Using words with specific reactions helps. In this case, the word "however" leads people to focus more on what was said after than what was said before. By bringing in logical points and behaving as if your opinion was completely without motive, your friend will likely opt for the haircut, and his girlfriend may even owe you a favor.

Change the Environment to Your Advantage

Studies have shown that the environment someone is in can have an impact on their decisions. This would come as a form of subliminal persuasion. For example, if you desperately need a study partner for an upcoming exam, you shouldn't ask your preferred partner in the mall. The mall is surrounded by fun activities, bright lights, music, and other distractions. However, if you were to ask him in an environment that stimulates the idea of studying in his brain, such as the library, he's more likely to agree with you. Better yet, if you can somehow work a pencil and a textbook into the atmosphere, you'll almost guarantee to win over his answer. Studies have shown that the brain works differently in different environments, which is why it can be difficult to recognize a co-worker or peer in a supermarket. If you want someone to make a business transaction, your success is more likely if there is a briefcase and a fountain pen within their vision, as these items tend to bring out the desire for money in people.

Speak Quickly

If you find yourself caught in an argument that you plan to win, speed up your speech. If you're speaking quickly, you sound more prepared with arguments, and your opponent has far less time to think of a coherent response, as he or she is focused on processing your arguments instead. The other person will become flustered in their confusion and trip up on their arguments. Eventually they will drop their side of the disagreement out of frustration and you will come out victorious. Watch for signs of irritation and frustration on their face. If you see these signs, you are close to winning.

Butter Them Up Ahead of Time

If you use subliminal persuasion and NLP to provide ideas that someone should do something or is excelled in a certain area you need them to be, they'll believe it. If you do this ahead of time, when the time comes for you to ask that favor or propose the idea, they will want to follow through. Remember the rules of subliminal persuasion, however. The ideas shouldn't appear to come from you. Point out objects that may put the idea in their head, or, play your reaction to awe whenever the idea of them doing the act is brought up. For example, if you want someone to paint your living room, you might steer them towards a creative environment and draw attention to a paint roller. You could pick it up and observe it, stand near it a moment, or even look at it for an extended length of time. If they take interest in the object, such as picking it up or looking at it thoughtfully, focus your reaction. Act interested in the idea of them painting a wall. Then, when you actually put in the request, refer to that moment and explain why you think they are perfect for the job. Environment, body language analysis, and subliminal persuasion all come into play here.

When in Doubt, Collect a Favor

As briefly mentioned in chapter one, no one likes to be indebted to someone. The easiest way to ask for a favor, is to provide one beforehand. If you aid someone's success in some way, or bail them out of a tough situation, they'll feel inclined to return this act of kindness later. If you've been painting yourself as an honest, genuine person as described in the tactic of NLP, the act will feel genuine. Those who have been given something from a generous person always feel the obligation to return the favor. It is best, however, to incorporate subliminal persuasion, and not to outright say that they owe you a favor. Nothing makes a kind act seem more benevolent than a selfless one without reciprocation. For example, you could begin the statement with, "Will you do me a favor?" Instead of outright asking them to do the favor. Because of the previous favor or favors you have done for them, they will answer before they even know what it is. This trick is especially useful if you believe they won't enjoy the request.

Shock Them

This can be done in multiple ways. One way to shock a person into complying, is to display what you know, or maybe what you don't, about them. This is an excellent chance to try out some cold reading and display your analysis skills. If you know a lot about someone, you must have paid attention and genuinely care. If you do this, and don't give the other time to think about the action that just occurred, they'll likely do as you suggest without an after-thought. Don't use this tactic often, however, as a shocking act isn't so shocking if it's done multiple times. As an example, you could surprise them with their favorite meal or make a comment on an interest of theirs that they mentioned in passing at one time.

Blackmail Exists

Often a desperate act that will likely lose the confidence you've built in someone is blackmail. Because it is so risky, and displays a mean streak, it is best to avoid blackmail all together. However, if you absolutely must, you have the skills to do so effectively. With cold reading, you can pull information from the person you wish to blackmail. An odd smudge of lipstick on your male friend's face, a lie you overheard someone speak that you could threaten to share or using a vague statement about something they could have did that you know nothing about, while allowing them to fill in the gaps and "realize" what you mean. These same tricks can be used under the category of earning a favor, however. You could hint that you noticed that lipstick or heard that lie, and promise you'll keep their secrets. You could also use the same trick of hinting you know what you really don't in this same way. Not only will you maintain the relationship you need to gain further favors from this person, but you won't earn a nasty reputation that could prevent further manipulation of other people. Remember, an important aspect of persuasion is to appear trustworthy.

What People do Subconsciously

A simple trick that I've personally used is to distract someone while you guide them to do something. These acts must be simple, and you'll need a little muscle memory on the other person's part. You could engage them in a conversation about something they are passionate about or interested in. Remain engaged in this conversation and keep them going. If you want them to hold something, open a door, or perform another simple task, you can guide them to the act while keeping the conversation going. Without realizing it, your companion will do as you wish subconsciously. It may not be an extravagant manipulation, but it can make your life simpler if you've gone shopping with this person and want them to carry the bags or want them to hold onto your coffee. Guiding them to the act has to remain subtle, as their focus must remain on the conversation. By the time they realize what has happened, the act is usually over, if they notice at all. For example, I know someone who has more passion about a video game in his little finger than most people have in their whole bodies for anything else. Walking to his house, I didn't feel like holding the bag I had taken with me. I casually brought up the conversation of this game and watched his eyes light up. His head became taller and his stance was more relaxed. As he began talking, I asked a few questions to keep him moving along. I watched for the opportunity when his hand extended to me while he explained a concept to me and I handed it to him. He didn't seem to notice as he continued describing a fictional race of elves with enthusiasm. He simply continued to hold the bag as he spoke all the way to his house. Had I asked him to hold my bag without using persuasion, he might have still done so, but there's still that chance that he wouldn't.

Switch it up

Switching up both word choices and sentence length will increase your chances of getting a "yes" for the request you are asking. Using "I" phrases instead of "you" phrases or "don't" instead of "can't" lead the person you're requesting to come to the conclusion themselves. This is a form of subliminal persuasion, as you don't outright ask what you want. For example, the sentence "Will you go to the department store?" Doesn't sound as appealing as "I am so exhausted, and I still have to go to the department store". If you play the victim and appear in need of aid, the other person might come to your rescue. This is especially true if you've done a favor for them recently. Switching up sentence length is both an author trick and a speaker trick as well to keep an audience engaged. If you alternate between long and brief sentences, your statement sounds more appealing to the ear, and you sound more certain. Authors will change up sentence lengths when describing a scene to give readers a break from the long sentences for a moment. It's difficult to follow a large block of word, even if it's spoken. It is also important to use appealing word descriptions instead of simple phrases. Convincing someone to eat organic foods is more possible if you use words such as "all natural" instead of the simple "healthy". This is why advertisements exclaim, usually in large letters, loaded descriptions of their product.

Mimic Body Language

Mentioned briefly in chapter one, mirroring a person's subtle body language is a persuasive technique that that can increase your chances of getting what you want. When someone sees familiarity in you, even at a subconscious level, they'll respond more positively to your requests. You can mirror a person's body language while using any other technique as well, so it may act as that cherry on top that will get you what you want. For example, if you have developed the needed rapport with this person, have set the environment as you need to, and yet you still feel like you need one extra push to drive the idea home for them, watch their movement and study the way they move. Do they toss their hair out of their eyes? Maybe they roll their shoulders often. Have they uncrossed and re-crossed their legs multiple times? Small movements that they don't realize they are doing should be the key focus when you copy their body language. If they see something of themselves in you, at a subconscious level, they will trust you more and will be more open to your suggestions.

Pay Attention

This may seem like an idea that's too simple, however it pays to pay attention to someone. If you've just listened to what the other person is saying and used your own body language to show that you were listening and interested just before you make your request, you are more likely to persuade them. People want to be heard. If they feel like you have listened and genuinely care about what they have to say, they'll be more responsive to you. You can do this by facing them with your body as they speak and make eye contact with them. Nod at appropriate times and ask questions. It's important to put your analysis skills to work in this moment as well. Are they responding positively to your efforts? Do they appear to be engaged in the conversation? Is their mood appropriate for the request? It won't work to your advantage to ask a favor of someone who has just told you about their favorite cat passing away. Keep the conversation light, but make sure the other person is engaged and cares about what they are saying.

Take Advantage of Confusion

Humans are habitual creatures. By nature, we all tend to follow some sort of routine, and when it falters, we scramble. When this happens, a person tends to cling to the closest action they can take in the midst of their confusion. If this has happened, and the person is a bit lost, you can take advantage of the moment to suggest a course of action that is preferable to you. They'll likely take any sort of direction they can get to go back on track, so they'll take the suggestion more easily than if they were clear-minded. Here is an example of this persuasive technique. Your friend always goes to a specific restaurant for lunch on Friday. This Friday, she has asked that you join her to catch up. You don't care much for the menu, and the last time you dined there you felt ill that night. However, your friend is adamant and you're both on your way. Luckily, she also drives the same direction to this restaurant every Friday. Today, there's an unexpected detour due to construction and your friend is visibly shocked. Now would be the time to suggest a different place. Speak calmly and suggest somewhere you can navigate to under these new circumstances. Your friend will oblige to escape the mess of confusion she's found herself in. You'll get your choice of restaurant, and your friend will thank you for being so helpful.

Lying

When using lying as a persuasive technique, it is best not to do so with someone who you have been building a relationship with. Lying is best used on someone whom you haven't built the basic NLP foundations with and likely never will. The reason is, those who know your baseline reaction and body language can spot the anxious behaviors of a lie much more easily than someone who has just met you. When lying, you'll need to utilize your cold reading and analysis skills more than NLP or subliminal persuasion, as these skills can be used from afar. Pay attention to their behavior and watch for their reactions. Is there suspicion written in their eyes? This can be seen as tension in the forehead, pursed lips, and slightly narrowed eyes. If they seem to believe your story, their face will hold interest. They won't be fidgeting and they might occasionally nod. It's important to pay attention to your own body language as well. Remember, when someone is leaning away from another, they are perceived as uncomfortable, and if they are hiding their hands in any way, they are hiding something. Try not to touch your hands together or hide them and keep your perceived mood light.

The Ellsberg Paradox

Known for leaking the Pentagon Papers, Daniel Ellsberg began his career by studying decision-making. His paradox is explained with an example of two urns. The first urn is full of black and red balls of an unknown ratio. There could be one black ball and the rest are red, it could be 50 of one and 50 of the other, no one knew. The second urn was, for certain, 50 of one and 50 of the other. People were asked to guess which color they would draw before choosing which urn to draw from.

Anyone who drew they guess would win $100 and anyone who guessed incorrectly would get nothing. What Ellsberg discovered was that most of the population chose to bet before drawing from the known urn.

What this explains, is that people tend to avoid risks. If you present a choice to someone, and provide all of the facts of one, and admit to some unknown factors to the other, they will likely choose the option that is complete, regardless of the facts. You can use this to your advantage if you want to sway their decision one way or another. A little deception and oversimplifying may be included in this tactic, so it is important to remember your body language and how it is perceived to the other person.

Group Influence

There is a reason companies will display their top reviews in a visible space on their website. People often base their decisions on statistics, even if it is a statistic based solely on the opinions of others and no science or evidence. If a group or people are willing to agree with you, that last person you are trying to persuade is likely to change their stance to match up with the majority vote. You can do this in a variety of ways, from persuading the others individually, or choosing people you already know will agree with you to back up your idea. Just as a group of sheep will follow each other, humans can fall into the group complex as well.

Present You High Selling Points First

In any situation, people tend to focus on the information they were given first the most. This is why gossip is frowned upon, as people are likely to believe the false rumors more than the facts, even if they were presented after. If the first point on your idea is a weak one, the other person may not follow through, even if the following points are logical and strong. Think about your word choice, and word order carefully before you present the idea. Use your other skills to ensure this person is open to a new idea and drive it home by offering the greatest benefits from the beginning. They will focus on that and are more likely to agree with you. This trick is best mixed with others, such as the favor exchange, the group complex, or overselling your idea.

Contrast Your Requests

Sometimes, if your request is large and will likely be difficult to persuade someone on, you can begin by making a smaller one in advance. If you ask someone to help you with a minor thing, such as making a run to the store for you, they may do so. After, you can ease your way up to the larger request you originally wanted to make, such as keeping a big secret for you or taking a big risk. Inversely, you can also make a small request seem simple and logical by first proposing a grand, likely ridiculous scheme. You could begin with something outrageous like streaking through a store or performing a grand heist. After

MANIPULATION AND DARK PSYCHOLOGY

your large idea is shot down, you can then attempt the smaller, less risky favor. Because the first one seemed beyond logical reasoning, the second option will appear reasonable in comparison, and the other person will be more inclined to comply. Stores and online shops use this trick in the form of a decoy sale. They may offer three options of a product. One is decently priced, the second is expensive, and the third is a combination of the two at the same price as the expensive option. Which one is the decoy? The expensive option is placed to increase the appeal of the third choice, making it look like a deal that it might not have seemed like before. Another version of this trick is when shops frequently have "sales" which actually contain the real price, with a much larger version of the price set as the original value. Who hasn't been a victim of this manipulation? It's hard to say no to a pack of fourteen pairs of socks when they are ten dollars off for a limited time.

Limited Time

Another tactic companies use that you can experiment with, is the limited time trick. It's hard to pass up something that states it only exists for a limited time, as the stress of never having such an opportunity again puts pressure on you. You can use this to your advantage and offer an opportunity to your friend as a chance that won't come again. For example, if you'd like your co-worker to call in sick on the same day as you, you might look up events that are happening on that day. If that co-worker refuses, or seems hesitant to join you, you can explain that there is a concert of only local bands playing at the park that day and they may never play again. Neither of you may be especially fond of local bands, however the fact that they may not come again will at least give your co-worker pause. If you can find a time sensitive occasion that appeals to the other person, you're even more likely to get what you want out of them. The more they hesitate before responding, the more they are considering the option. Remember, it is also beneficial to begin with the selling points. So, don't begin your request with, "I know we might get fired, but let's skip work tomorrow!"

The "But You're Free" Technique

People like choices. Having the freedom to choose between different options, or to not opt for an option at all, make them feel more in control of a situation and more likely to agree. If you wish to sway someone to do something specific, you may present it as an option. Use your other skills and sell the idea. Make is sound plausible and apply how it will benefit the other person just as much, or more than you. Watch their reactions and see if you have caught their interest. If all goes well, then you can drive the idea home by using a magic statement at the end. "But you're free not to". As it is a choice option, people will respond more positively and will often opt to perform the action based on the fact that they have the choice. Of course, they likely had the choice to begin with. This is why psychology works so well, because the brain and mind can be tricked.

Use a Relatable Experience

I had provided an example of this experience in chapter one, when I persuaded a friend to visit her father by providing her with a story of my own, similar experience. Sometimes, people want reassurance that they aren't alone in a situation. If you provide some common ground and explain an anecdote that is relatable to the situation that has a positive outcome, the other person is more inclined to agree to follow through with theirs. If you are pushing someone to take a risky job, explain a time when you took a risk and how it benefited you. Success stories drive a lot of people to take chances. Remember, people don't like to take risks about the unknown. So, provide them with information to base their decision on.

It Worked Before, It'll Work Again

Many people believe that if something worked well in their favor, the streak will continue on. Gambling is a business that preys on this belief, as people who are lucky enough to win at a game will lose all of their winnings on pushing that luck and playing again. You can use it to your advantage as well, especially if you want someone to do something that they, or another person, has attempted before with success. If you remind this person that the previous situation was favorable, they are more likely to comply with your logic. Of course, if this action was based on luck, such as the gambling is, the chances of it turning out as favorable has no correlation with the previous outcome. However, the other person may not know that fact, as many don't.

Conclusion

Thank you for making it through to the end of *Manipulation: Dark Psychology- How to Analyze People and Influence Them to Do Anything You Want Using NLP and Subliminal Persuasion*, I hope it was informative and able to provide you with all of the tools you need to persuade people to do as you wish without them even being aware, and to make the psychological choices appropriate for each unique situation.

The next step is to take all of the information you learned here and put it to use in any way you wish. Remember that to manipulate someone isn't always to take advantage of them. This power can do another a favor as much as it can be immoral. Regardless, how you choose to do so is up to only you. Remember that knowing the process of NLP will get you in and allow you to manipulate someone. Understanding subliminal persuasion will grant you subtlety and provide that edge you need to give them the idea without them even knowing it wasn't theirs. Practice some cold reading to surprise and learn even more about a person so you can get whatever you desire. Whether as a parlor trick to get some extra money, or to obtain information. Don't forget the knowledge of analyzing people, as it will ensure you'll achieve your goals. Remember the rules of persuasion, which is to remember to observe and appear trustworthy. Without reading body language and behavior at least, you won't be as successful in persuasion with the rest of the knowledge you've gained. Finally, put all of these skills together to achieve the ultimate persuasion tactic, however you choose to use it.

Thank you

Before you go, I just wanted to say thank you for purchasing my book.

You could have picked from dozens of other books on the same topic but you took a chance and chose this one.

So, a HUGE thanks to you for getting this book and for reading all the way to the end.

Now I wanted to ask you for a small favor. **Could you please take just a few minutes to leave a review for this book?**

This feedback will help me continue to write the type of books that will help you get the results you want. So if you enjoyed it, please let me know.

* 9 7 8 1 9 5 1 4 2 9 4 9 2 *